Electricity and Electronics - 3

OPERATIONAL AMPLIFIERS

AND OTHER SPECIAL DEVICES

THEORY, PRACTICE AND SOLVED AND PROPOSED EXERCISES

ALBEIRO PATIÑO BUILES

Electricity and Electronics - 3

OPERATIONAL AMPLIFIERS

AND OTHER SPECIAL DEVICES

THEORY, PRACTICE AND SOLVED AND PROPOSED EXERCISES

Science and Technology

XALAMBO
EDITORIAL

Collection *Science and Technology*
OPERATIONAL AMPLIFIERS
AND OTHER SPECIAL DEVICES
© Albeiro Patiño Builes, 2023
© Xalambo Editorial, 2023

1st edition: June 2023
ISBN: 978-958-53954-9-7

Editorial Direction: Albeiro Patiño Builes
Technical Review and Layout: David Esteban Londoño Patiño
Cover design: David Esteban Londoño Patiño
Translation: David Esteban Londoño Patiño

Edited in Medellín, Colombia
Xalambo Editorial
www.xalambo.com
Tel.: (57) 302 827 35 13

«It is not enough to have good ingenuity; the main thing is to apply it well».

Rene Descartes

INDEX

Chapter 1

THE DIFFERENTIAL AMPLIFIER

Introduction

In electronics, the term "discrete" is used to denote individual elements and circuits made up of individual components such as transistors, diodes, resistors, etc. Generally, a discrete circuit is one whose components have been soldered or connected together in some way. For a long time, these circuits were especially useful. However, in the 1960s, they were largely replaced by integrated circuits (ICs), which eliminated the need for mechanical connection of discrete elements. An integrated circuit is a device that has its own transistors and resistors. These components are not discrete, but rather integrated, meaning they are produced and connected during the manufacturing process, which has made possible the increasingly amazing process of miniaturization.

Types of integrated circuits

Currently, a large number of circuits are produced as integrated circuits, which come in several types: monolithic, thin-film, thick-film, and hybrid.

The monolithic IC is the most common type of integrated circuit. Commercial models available can be used as amplifiers, voltage regulators, switches, AM receivers, television circuits, and computer circuits. The disadvantage they present is that they are of limited power, usually less than 1W.

For higher powers, thin-film and thick-film ICs are available. They are larger than monolithic ones, and passive components such as resistors and capacitors are integrated, but transistors and diodes are connected as discrete components to form a complete circuit. Therefore, these thin-film and thick-film components are a combination of integrated and discrete components.

In high power applications, hybrid ICs are used. These combine two or more monolithic ICs into a single circuit or combine monolithic ICs with thin-film and thick-film circuits. They are widely used in applications ranging from 5W to over 50W.

Integration scales

Depending on the number of elements in a single IC, there are diverse levels of integration. In the Small-Scale Integration (SSI) level, there are less than 12 integrated components in a single circuit. Most SSI chips use integrated resistors, diodes, and bipolar transistors.

The Middle Scale Integration (MSI) refers to ICs that have 12 to 100 integrated components per chip. Most of these MSI ICs use bipolar components or MOSFET transistors. Large Scale Integration (LSI) refers to ICs with more than 100 components. The majority of LSI chips are of the MOS type.

The Differential Amplifier

In a chip, transistors, diodes, and resistors are the practical components that can be produced. Capacitors manufactured in a chip have exceptionally low capacity, usually less than 50pF. That is, ICs do not use coupling and decoupling capacitors. Instead, monolithic IC stages are directly coupled, without a capacitor. One of the best direct-coupling stages is the differential amplifier. This is widely used as the input stage of an operational amplifier. For this reason, studying the differential amplifier and its properties will also involve studying the input characteristics of the common operational amplifier.

In general terms, an amplifier is an electronic circuit that contains BJT and FET devices, usually packaged in ICs, which provides voltage or current gain. It can also provide power gain or allow impedance transformation.

Amplifiers can be classified in many ways. There are low-frequency amplifiers, audio amplifiers, ultrasonic amplifiers, radio frequency (RF) amplifiers, broadband amplifiers, video amplifiers, each type operating in a prescribed frequency range.

General form

Figure 1.1 shows the diagram based on discrete components of a differential amplifier. It has two inputs, V_{i1} and V_{i2}. Since there are no coupling capacitors, signals of any frequency can be used, including DC or zero-frequency signals. The output signal is the voltage measured between the collectors of the transistors. The circuit is symmetrical with identical transistor and collector resistors, which is why, if equal input signals are applied, the output will be zero. When V_{i1} is greater than V_{i2}, an output voltage with the shown polarity appears. When V_{i1} is less than V_{i2}, the output voltage has the opposite polarity.

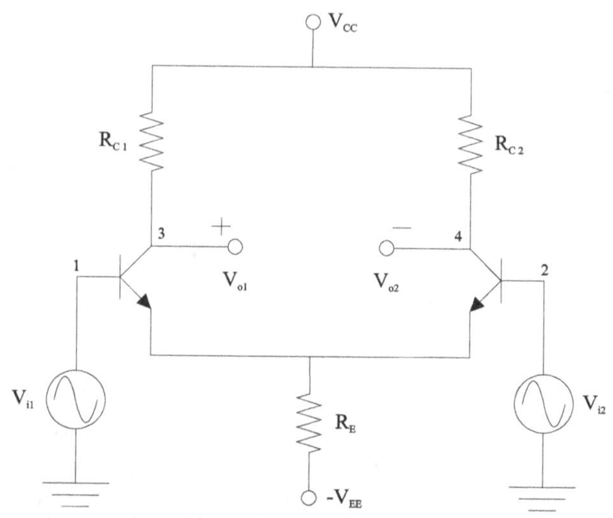

Figure 1-1. Differential amplifier.

The commonly used symbol to represent the differential amplifier is shown in Figure 1.2.

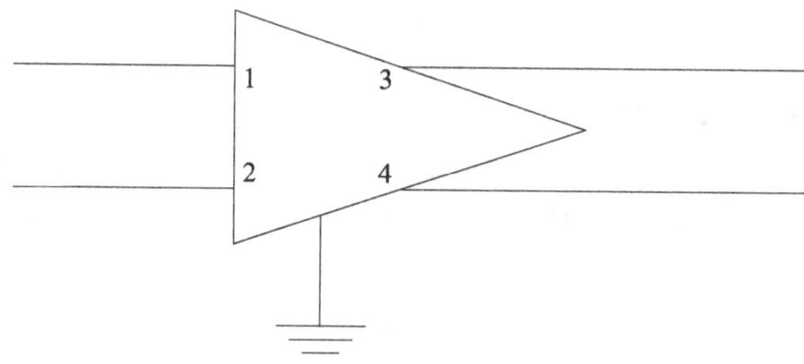

Figure 1-2. Block diagram of a differential amplifier.

The two separate inputs (1 and 2) and two separate outputs (3 and 4) are shown. Note that in Figure 1.2, a separate ground connection is shown because both input and output terminals can be different from ground. Voltages can be applied to both input terminals and output voltages appear on both output terminals. However, there are specific polarities for both input and output terminals.

Differential amplifier with input on one terminal only

Consider the operation of the differential amplifier with a single input signal applied to terminal 1, with terminal 2 connected to ground (0V).

In Figure 1.3 (a) and (b), the circuit and block diagram can be seen for the case of having an input signal V_{i1} at terminal 1 and the output V_{o1} at terminal 3.

A sinusoidal input and an inverted amplified output are observed. The circuit diagram shows the sinusoidal input applied to the base of a transistor and the amplified and inverted output at the collector terminal.

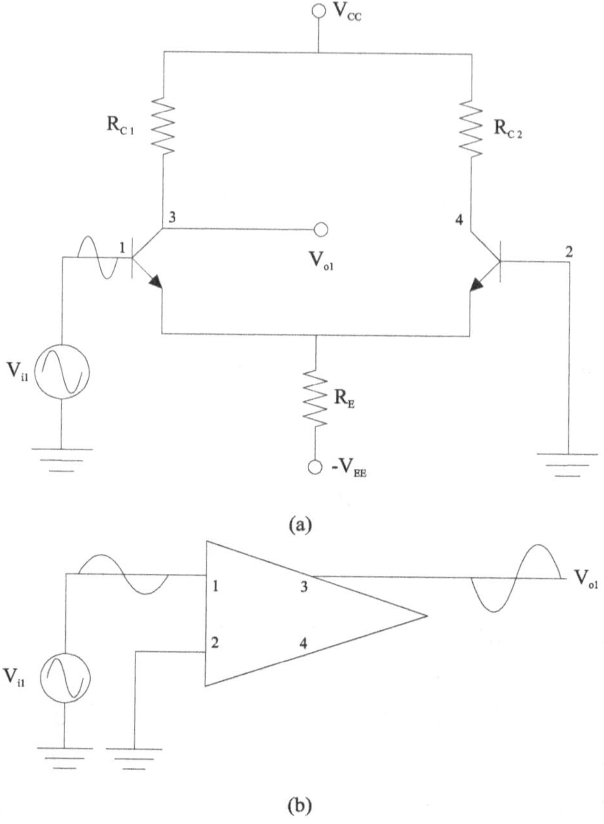

(a)

(b)

Figure 1-3. Diagram (a) Circuit diagram and (b) block diagram with single input differential amplifier.

The fact that the output 4 is not considered does not mean that there is no signal at that output. On the contrary, in the circuit of Figure 1.4, the operation of the differential amplifier can be seen with the enabled output V_{o2} at terminal 4. This signal is still due to the input V_{i1} at terminal 1, and the output signal V_{o2} at terminal 4 is an in-phase signal with the V_{i1} signal and amplified with respect to it.

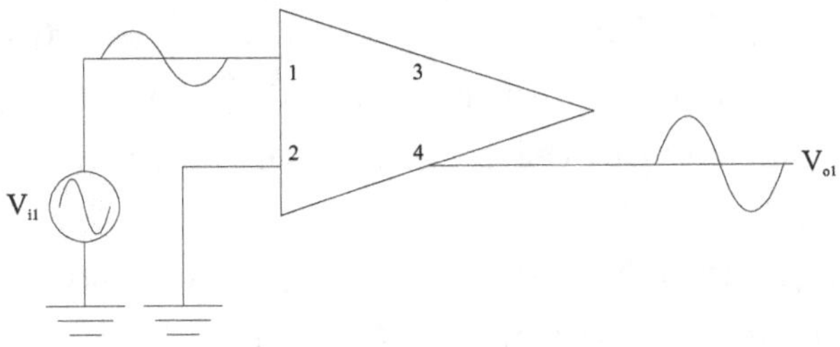

Figure 1-4. Output signal V_{o1} due to the input signal V_{i1} in a differential amplifier.

Because the emitter resistor is connected in common with both emitters, a voltage due to V_{i1} appears at the common emitter point (Figure 1.5). This sinusoidal voltage measured with respect to ground is approximately half in magnitude and in phase with V_{i1}, as it results from the action of an emitter follower in this circuit.

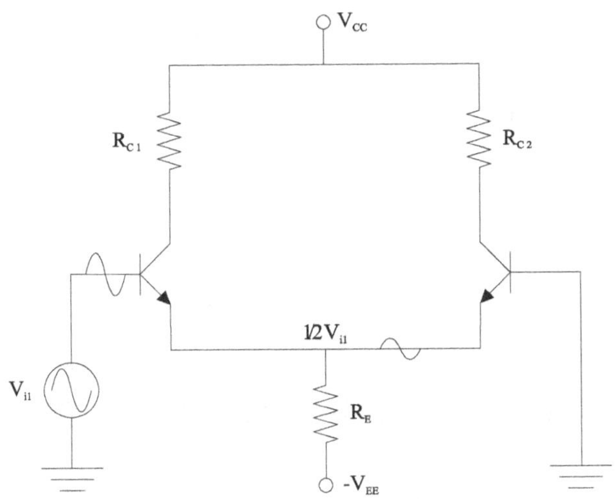

Figure 1-5. Voltage at the emitter resistor.

In conclusion, the input at terminal 1 produces output signals at both terminals 3 and 4. Furthermore, these outputs have opposite polarities and are of approximately the same magnitude. Finally, the output at terminal 4 has the same polarity as the input at terminal 1, while the output at terminal 3 has the opposite polarity of the input at terminal 1 (figure 1.6 (a)).

As a consequence of all the details previously mentioned, a signal applied to terminal 2 (with terminal 1 grounded) will result in output voltages as shown in figure 1.6(b).

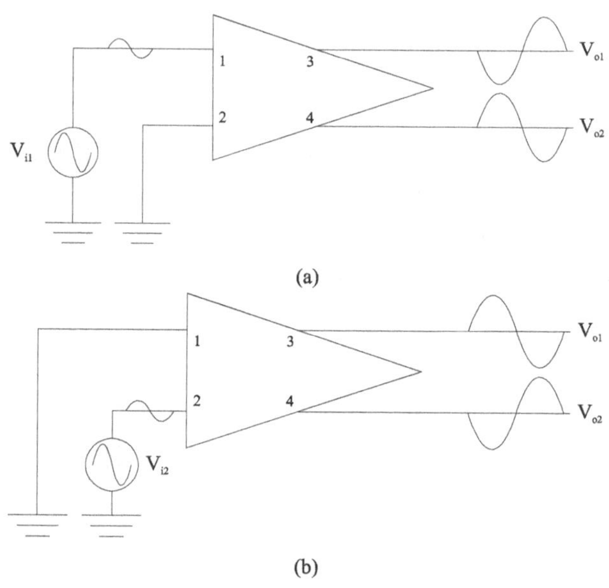

Figure 1-6. Single input, opposite polarity outputs.

Operation with differential input (double input)

The operation of the differential amplifier is not limited to having one channel connected to a signal and the other to ground. Rather, it is possible to apply signals to each of the input terminals, with outputs of opposite polarity appearing at the output terminals. The normal use of differential mode with dual input is when the two signals have opposite polarities and possess the same magnitude. (Figure 1.7).

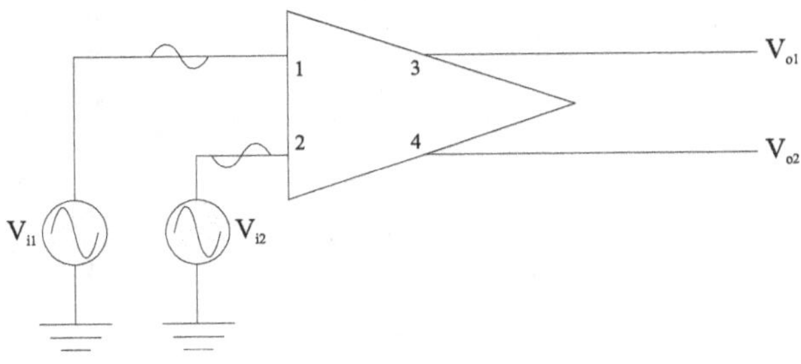

Figure 1-7. Operation with differential input signal.

To study this circuit, we apply the superposition principle and observe the output signals due to each input signal separately. Figures 1.8 (a) and (b) show this fact, and Figure 1.8 (c) presents the output signal at each terminal with both input signals enabled. Note how the output signal at each terminal in Figure 1.8 (c) is twice the output signal at each terminal in Figures 1.8 (a) and (b).

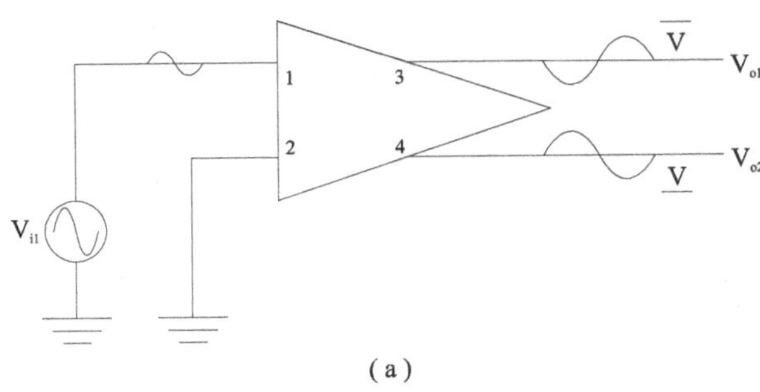

(a)

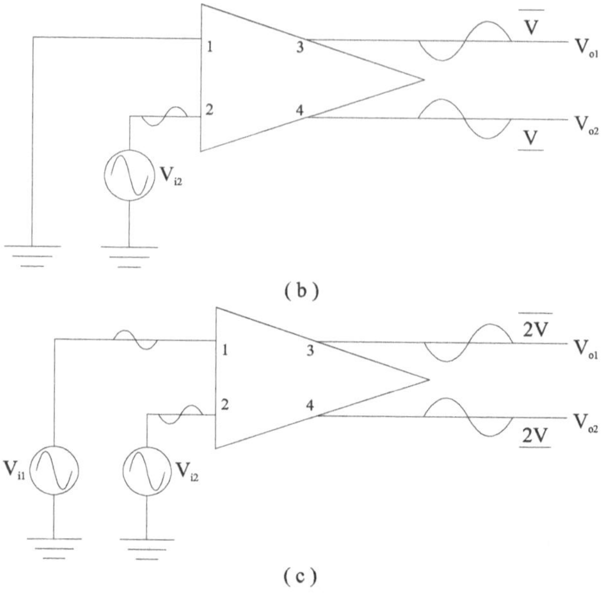

Figure 1-8. Differential operation of the amplifier a) Vi2=0, b) Vi1=0, c) Both inputs are present.

The input applied to terminal 1 results in an amplified output of opposite polarity at terminal 3 and an amplified output of the same polarity at terminal 4. Assuming the inputs are of the same magnitude and the output magnitudes are approximately equal, each output will have a peak value of V.

The input applied to terminal 2 results in an amplified output of opposite polarity at terminal 4 and an amplified output of the same polarity at terminal 3. The magnitudes of the outputs will be V since the input magnitudes were assumed to be approximately equal. It is noted that the corresponding outputs in the circuits of Figures 1.8(a) and (b) have the same polarity. By superposition, these signals can be added to obtain the total operation of the circuit shown in Figure 1.8(c). The output of each terminal is twice that resulting from the operation of a single input because the input signals have opposite polarity.

If the applied inputs had the same polarity (or if the same input were applied to both terminals), the resulting signals due to each input, acting alone, would be of opposite polarity at each of the outputs, and the resulting output would ideally be zero volts (0V), as shown in figure 1.9.

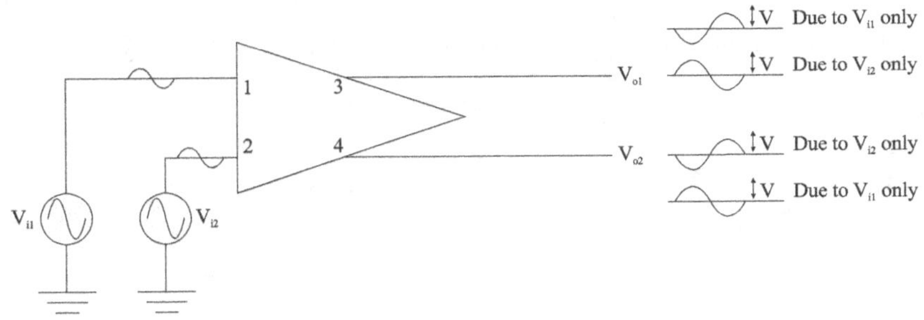

Figure 1-9. Operation with in-phase input signals.

Let us consider the connection of two differential amplifiers as shown in figure 1.10. As mentioned before, if the amplifiers had the same gain, with a single input, the outputs of stage 1 would be greater than the input by an amount equal to the amplifier gain, while the outputs of stage 2 would be larger than the inputs to stage 2 by a factor equal to the gain. The initial signal from a radio antenna, a record player pickup, etc. is of a single terminal and will be used as such in this case. However, the second differential amplifier stage could be operated with two inputs to obtain twice the gain of the stage.

Any output from stage 2 (or both) could then be used as the amplified signal for the next section of the system. Although differential operation requires approximately equal signals of opposite polarity, these are generally available, especially after the gain of a single-input stage.

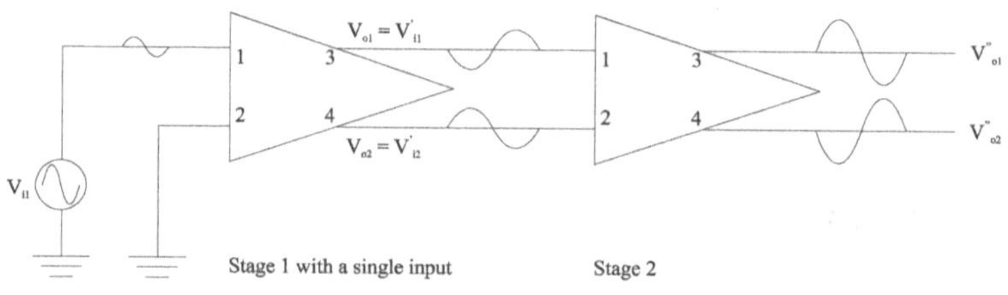

Figure 1-10. Single and dual operation of differential amplifier stages.

REVIEW

Concepts

Define or discuss the following:

- Discrete component.
- Integrated component.
    - o Monolithic integrated circuit.
    - o Thin-film and thick-film ICs.
    - o Hybrid ICs.
- High, medium, and low integration scales.
- Differential amplifier.
- Differential amplifier operating with a single input.
- Differential amplifier operating with dual input.

EXERCISES

1.1. Analyze the circuit in figure 1.11 and determine the waveforms at the differential amplifier outputs.

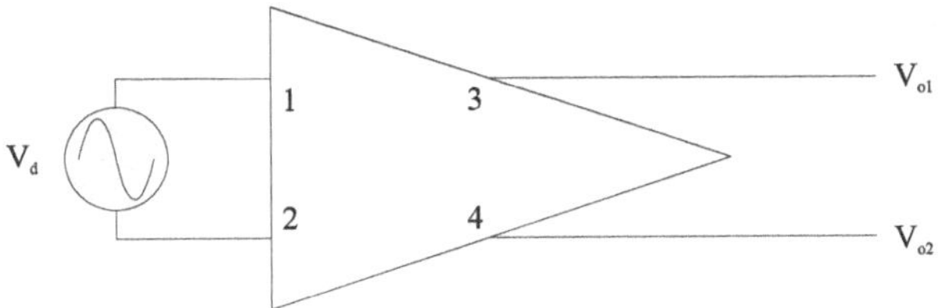

Figure 1-11. Circuit of exercise 1.1.

1.2. Analyze the circuit in Figure 1.12 and determine the waveforms at the outputs of the differential amplifier.

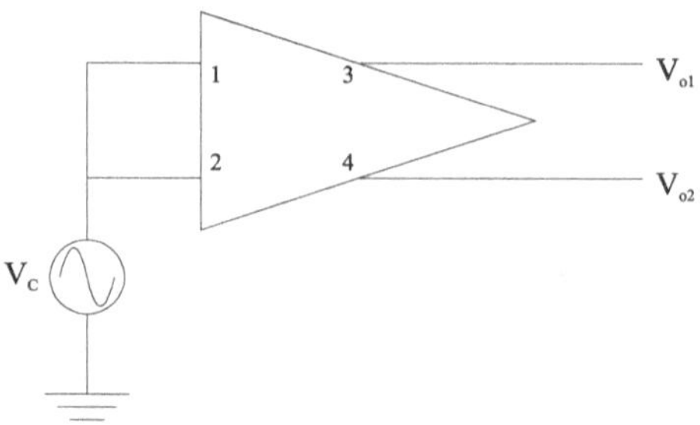

Figure 1-12. Circuit of exercise 1.2.

1.3. Analyze the circuit in figure 1.13 given the indicated input signal and determine the signals at the collectors and common emitter output.

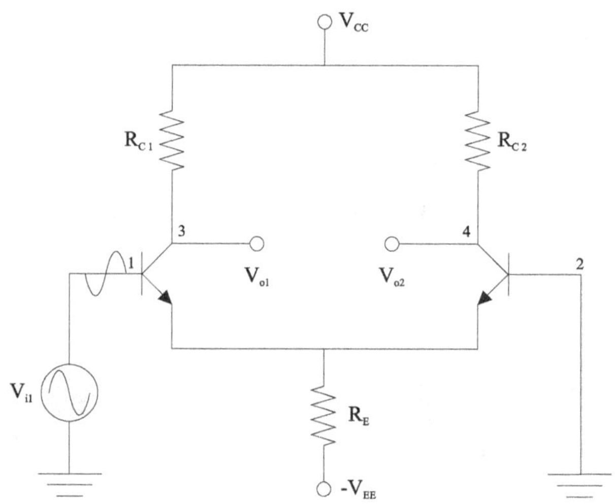

Figure 1-13. Circuit of exercise 1.3.

1.4. Determine the waveforms appearing at the terminals 3 and 4 of the differential amplifier shown in Figure 1.14.

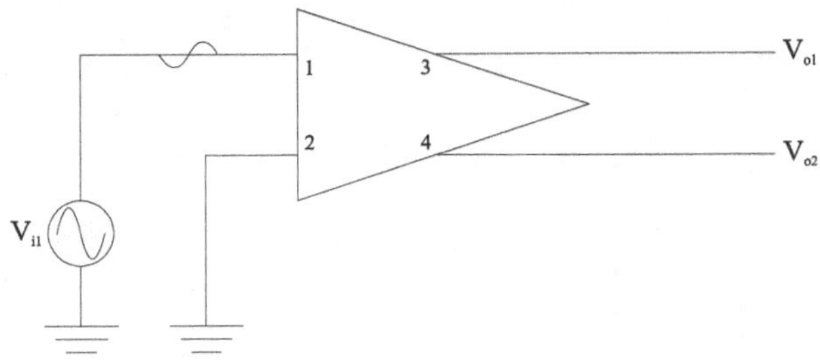

Figure 1-14. Circuit of exercise 1.4.

1.5. Given the circuit shown in figure 1.16, determine the waveforms at the outputs of the differential amplifiers in the distinct stages.

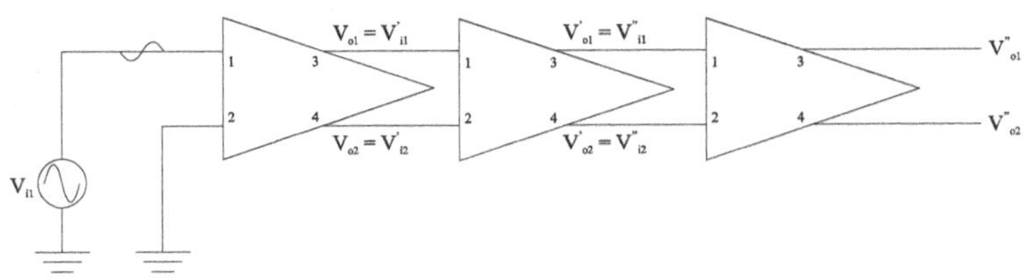

Figure 1-15. Circuit of exercise 1.5.

Chapter 2
THE OPERATIONAL AMPLIFIER

Constitution of the operational amplifier

An operational amplifier is a circuit in an IC package that is obtained by using multiple differential amplifiers.

The differential amplifier seen in the previous chapter is, therefore, a basic circuit used in the practical construction of operational amplifier units. Among the basic characteristics of this circuit are high voltage gain, high input resistance, and low output resistance. In Figure 2.1, an integrated circuit 347 can be seen which contains four operational amplifier units.

Currently, the Op-Amp 741 has become an industrial standard. In 1965, Fairchild Semiconductor introduced the μA709, the first widely used operational amplifier.

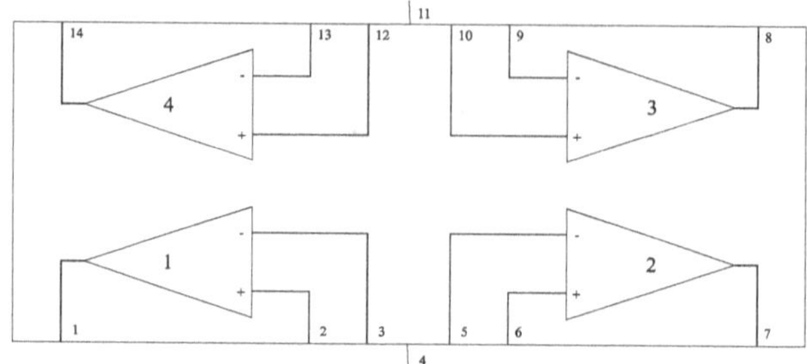

Figure 2-1. Integrated circuit 347.

In its early days, the μA709 had enormous success but had many disadvantages, which led to the appearance of the μA741. The μA741 has been widely accepted due to its ease of use and low cost. Several versions are now available in the market, including the Motorola MC1741, National Semiconductor LM741, and Texas Instruments SN72741, all of which are equivalent to the μA741 since they have the same specifications. Generally, all of these amplifiers are known as the 741.

It is worth mentioning that the 741 has different numbered versions: 741, 741A, 741C, 741E, 741N, and others. The difference between them lies in their voltage, temperature range, noise level, and other characteristics. The 741C (C standing for Commercial) is the cheapest and most widely used. It has an input impedance of 2MΩ, a voltage gain of 100,000, and an output impedance of 75Ω.

Some current uses for linear op-amps are in the fields of process control, communications, signal generators and power, displays, and test and measurement systems.

Experience with a linear Op Amp should focus on its most important fundamental properties. Accordingly, the objectives of this chapter will be to identify each terminal of the Op Amp and learn its purpose, some of its electrical limitations, and how to apply it with usefulness.

Operational amplifiers have five basic terminals: two for power supply, two for input signals, and one for output. Internally they are complex, however, it is not necessary to know anything about the internal operation of the Op. Amp. to use it.

In figure 2.2, four common packages are shown. As seen from the top, the terminals are counted in a counterclockwise direction. Terminal 1 is identified by a notch in the DIP of figure 2.2 (c) and (d) and by a dot in the flat package of figure 2.2 (b). Terminal 8 is identified by a metal tab in the tin-lead package of figure 2.2 (a).

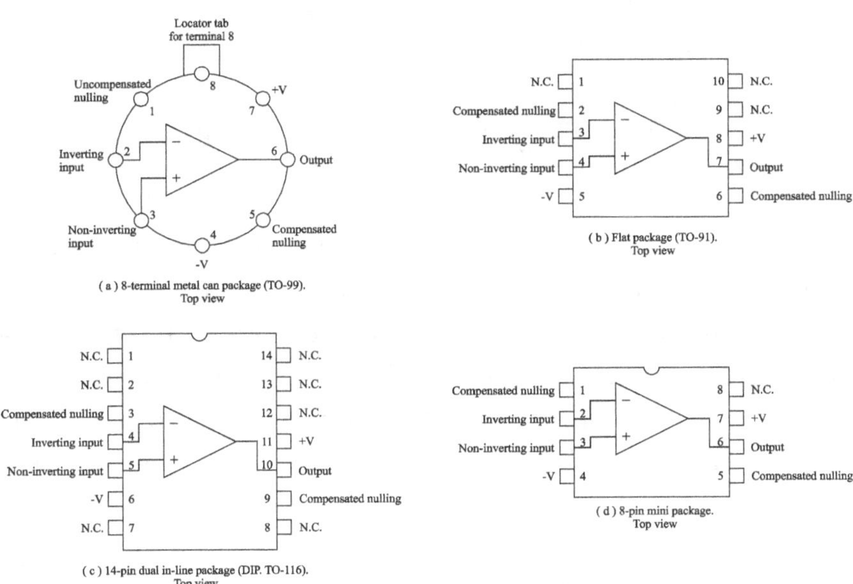

Figure 2-2. Connection diagram for typical Op. Amp. The abbreviation N.C. stands for "No Connection", i.e., there is no internal connection in the Op. Amp.

Operational Amplifier Terminals

The schematic circuit for the Op Amp is a triangle head, as shown in Figure 2.3. The triangle head symbolizes amplification and points from the input to the output.

Power supply terminals

The terminals of the Op Amp labeled as +V and -V identify the pins to which the power supply must be connected.

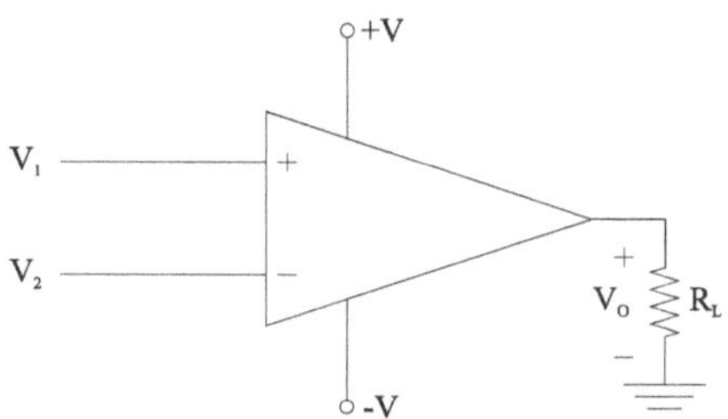

Figure 2-3. Op. Amp. power supply terminals.

The power supply in figure 2.3 is called bipolar, split, or dual and has typical values of ±15V, ±12V, and ±6V. Some special-purpose op-amps may require non-symmetric supplies, such as +12V and -6V, or even a single-polarity supply such as +30V and ground. The maximum supply voltage that can be applied between +V and -V is typically 36V or ±18V.

Output terminal

The output voltage, V_o, is measured with respect to ground. This output terminal is called a "single-ended output" since it is the only one present. The current limit that can be drawn from the output of an Op Amp is typically 5 to 10mA. The output voltage limit is determined by the supply voltage and the output transistors of the internal circuitry of the operational amplifier. These transistors require a collector-to-emitter voltage of 1 to 2V to ensure they operate as amplifiers and not as switches. Therefore, the output at the terminal will drop 2V from +V and 2V from -V. The upper limit of V_o is called the "positive saturation voltage," $+V_{sat}$, and the lower limit is called the "negative saturation voltage," $-V_{sat}$. For example, with a ±15V supply, $+V_{sat} = +13V$ and $-V_{sat} = -13V$. Thus, V_o is limited to a peak-to-peak variation of ±13V. Both the current and voltage limits impose a limit on the load resistance, R_L, of 2KΩ.

Some operational amplifiers, such as the LM741, have internal circuitry that automatically limits the current at the output terminal. Even in the case of a short circuit at the load resistor (R_L), the output current is limited to around 25mA. This feature prevents the destruction of the operational amplifier in the event of a short circuit.

EXAMPLE 2.1.

Given the circuit in Figure 2.4, analyze the conditions at the amplifier output.

SOLUTION

The maximum output current, including short circuit, is 25mA. We are biasing with ±13V, so the maximum output without clipping the waveform will be ±11V. Since we have a load resistor and an LED at the output, we assume an output bias current of 15mA. With this value and the voltage, we can calculate the load resistance, R_L.

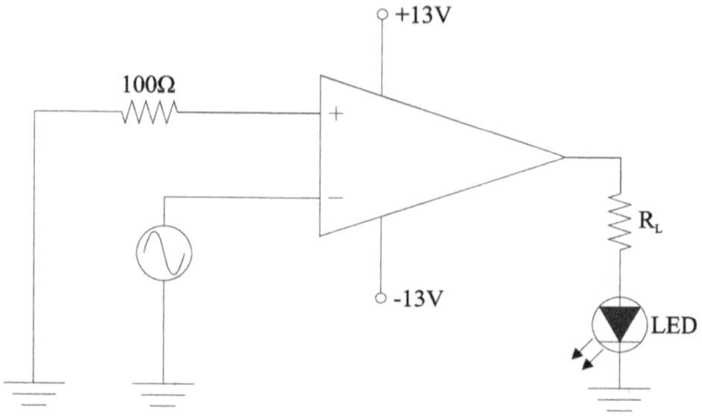

Figure 2-4. Circuit of example 2.1.

$$R_L = \frac{11V}{15mA} = \frac{11V}{15(10^{-3})A} = 750\Omega$$

The power that this resistor must dissipate is given by:

$$P = I^2 R_L = (15mA)^2(750\Omega)$$

That is to say:

$$P = 0.1125W$$

That means we can choose a 750Ω resistor with ¼W.

Input terminals

In Figure 2.3, there are two input terminals marked with "-" and "+". They are called differential input terminals because the output voltage, V_o, depends on the voltage difference between them, V_d, and the gain of the amplifier, G.

The polarity of the output signal is the same as the polarity of the input signal if it is applied to the terminal marked with (+). The polarity of the output signal is opposite or inverted with respect to the polarity of the input signal if it is applied to the terminal marked with (-). For these reasons, the (-) input is called the inverting input, and the (+) input is called the non-inverting input.

It is emphasized that the polarity of V_0 depends solely on the voltage difference between the inverting and non-inverting inputs. This voltage difference can be found as:

$$V_d = V_1 - V_2 \qquad (2.1)$$

Both input voltages are measured with respect to ground.

One important characteristic of the input terminals is the high impedance between them and also between each input terminal and ground.

Open circuit voltage gain

If the input differential voltage, V_d, is sufficiently small, the output voltage, V_o, will be determined by both V_d and the open-loop voltage gain, G. G is called "open-loop voltage gain" because the possible feedback connections from the output terminal to the input terminals have been left open. (Figure 2.5).

Consequently, V_o can be ideally expressed by the relationship:

$$V_o = GV_d \qquad (2.2)$$

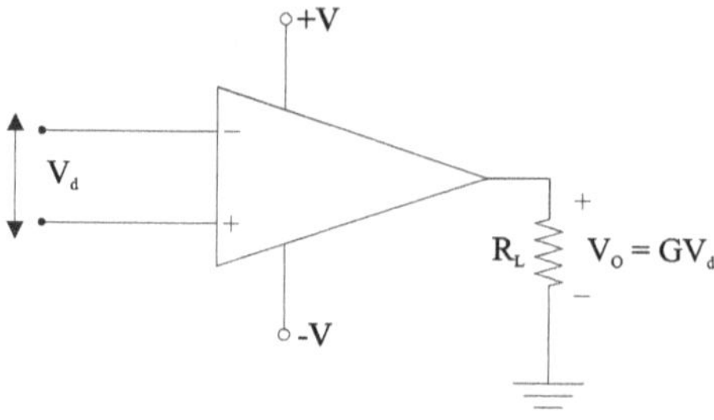

Figure 2-5. Schematic diagram for open-circuit voltage gain.

Input differential voltage, *Vd*

As hinted at the beginning of this chapter, the value of G is extremely large, often 100,000, 200,000, or higher, depending on the device's specification. Remember that V_o can never exceed the positive or negative saturation voltages, $+V_{sat}$ and $-V_{sat}$. For a power supply of ±15V, the saturation voltages would be approximately ±13V.

EXAMPLE 2.2

An operational amplifier has a power supply of ±15V. Determine the maximum output voltage that can be obtained without clipping the signal, and the input voltage at each terminal required to achieve it. The differential gain is 200,000.

SOLUTION

From equation (2.2) we have that the input voltage is given:

$$V_d = \frac{V_o}{G}$$

As the bias voltage is ±15V, the saturation voltage will be ±13V. The gain is 200000, so replacing it in the above equation we have:

$$V_{dmáx} = \frac{+V_{sat}}{G} = \frac{13V}{200000} = 65\mu V$$

And analogously:

$$-V_{dmáx} = \frac{-V_{sat}}{G} = \frac{-13V}{200000} = -65\mu V$$

That is to say, a voltage of ±65μV yields an output of ±13V.

In the laboratory, it is difficult to measure this voltage (65μV) due to signal noise, which can reach up to 1000μV. Additionally, measuring remarkably high gains is challenging. The imbalance of the voltage V_d also introduces errors.

Definition of terms for Operational Amplifiers

- VOLTAGE GAIN, DIFFERENTIAL - VOLTAGE GAIN FOR LARGE SIGNALS.

It is the rate of change in the output voltage at any output terminal with respect to ground, with respect to the difference in input voltages. A value of 106dB at some frequency is specified by manufacturers as the gain from an input terminal to any output terminal. The gain is specified by the manufacturer in units of decibels (dB). The relationship between decibels and gain as a numerical ratio of output voltage (V_o) to input voltage (V_i) is:

$$G_{dB} = 20\,log|G| = 20\,log\left|\frac{V_o}{V_i}\right| \qquad (2.3)$$

EXAMPLE 2.3

An operational amplifier has an output of 1V when a signal of 1mV is applied to one of its input terminals. Calculate the gain in dB.

SOLUTION

The gain is given by:

$$G = \frac{V_o}{V_i}$$

With $V_o = 1V$ and $V_i = 1mV$, we substitute and obtain:

$$G = \frac{1V}{10^{-3}V} = 1000$$

And replacing this value in equation (2.1)

$$G_{dB} = 20\,log|1000| = 20(3) = 60dB$$

EXAMPLE 2.4

Calculate the value of the dimensionless voltage gain corresponding to a gain of 106dB.

SOLUTION

If we use the formula given in equation (2.3), with $G_{dB} = 106dB$:

$$106 = 20\,log|G|$$

$$5.3 = \log|G|$$

$$|G| = \text{antilog}(5.3) = (2)(10^5) = 200000$$

- ### SINGLE-TERMINAL INPUT RESISTANCE (R_{in})

The input resistance of a single terminal is the ratio of the change in input voltage to the change in input current measured at any input terminal with respect to ground. A specified value of $10^{12}\Omega$ indicates a high value, which is important when connecting a source; if the input resistance is not larger than the source resistance, the load will cause the input voltage to be less than the signal voltage without load, resulting in a lower output voltage.

Bipolar operational amplifiers typically provide input resistances around 1MΩ, while BiFET operational amplifiers are specified at $10^{12}\Omega$ and BiMOS typically have $10^{15}\Omega$.

- ### OUTPUT RESISTANCE (R_o)

The output resistance is the ratio of the change in output voltage to the change in output current measured at the output terminal with respect to ground. The output resistance, typically around 100Ω, depends on the output stage used to drive the signal to the load.

- ### BALANCED VOLTAGE (V_{os})

It is the difference in DC voltages that must be applied to the input terminals to obtain equal operating voltages (zero output voltage) at the output terminal. It can also be defined as the required differential DC voltage between the inputs of an operational amplifier to force the output to 0V. Ideally, the value of V_{os} (offset voltage) should be 0V, and in practice, the value of V_{os} is only a few millivolts. When the Op Amp is primarily used for large-signal operation, a small balanced voltage is acceptable. However, in applications where a small output voltage represents a measured quantity, such as in a converter, meter, or measuring device, any non-zero voltage can result in a substantial error. In such circuit applications, an Op Amp with a small offset voltage should be used, or one that has input terminals that allow for adjusting the offset voltage. Later on, we will see in detail how to balance the input voltage.

- INPUT BIAS CURRENT

To ensure proper operation of the circuit inside the IC, sufficient DC bias current must be provided, as specified by the manufacturer's information. For BJT inputs, the required current is typically in the microampere range; for JFET input stages, the required current is in the few pico-ampere range.

- BALANCED INPUT CURRENT (I_{os})

The balanced input current is the difference in the currents at the two input terminals. The small difference in the bias currents at the inputs is amplified by the amplifier's gain to provide a balanced output voltage. The balanced current for BJT input circuits is in the order of nanoamperes, while for JFET input stages it is typically in the range of picoamperes.

- QUISCENT OPERATING VOLTAGE

Is the DC voltage at the output terminal with respect to ground.

- DC POWER DISSIPATION OF THE DEVICE

It is the total power dissipated by the device with no applied signal and no extreme load current.

- COMMON MODE VOLTAGE GAIN

It is the ratio of the signal voltage developed at the output terminal to the signal voltage applied to the input terminals connected in parallel.

- MAXIMUM OUTPUT VOLTAGE, $V_{o\,(p-p)}$

It is the maximum peak-to-peak output voltage measured with respect to ground that can be achieved without distorting the shape of a signal.

- RATE OF VOLTAGE CHANGE (SR-Slew Rate)

It is a parameter of the device that indicates how quickly the output voltage changes over time. A typical value is $13V/\mu s$.

Other characteristics of the Operational Amplifiers

As previously stated in section 2.2, the electrical symbol of an amplifier is an arrowhead. (Figure 2.6)

In figure 2.6, G represents the gain. The non-inverting input is V_1 and the inverting input is V_2.

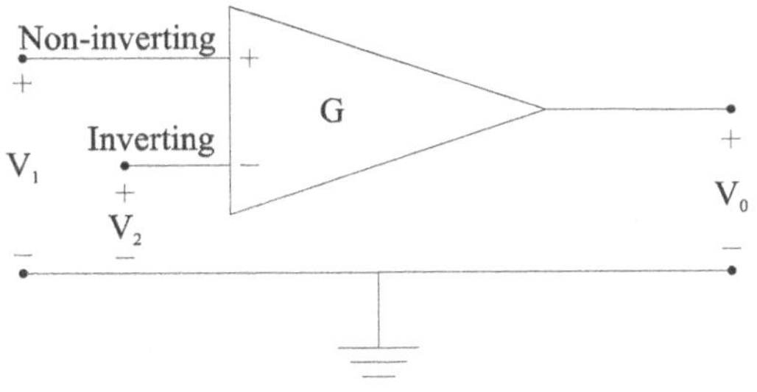

Figure 2-6. Electrical symbol of the operational amplifier.

The voltages V_1, V_2, and V_o are always measured with respect to ground, as shown in figure 2.6; and the input voltage is the differential voltage, given by equation (2.1), that is, $V_{in} = V_d$.

Most of the time, it is not necessary to draw the ground symbol as shown in Figure 2.6, but rather work with the symbol shown in Figure 2.7.

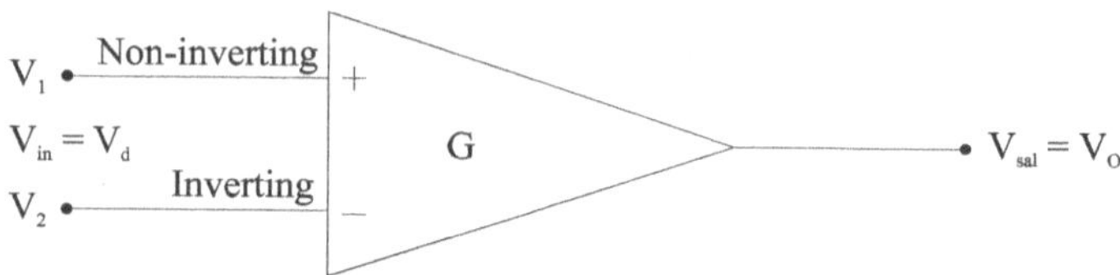

Figure 2-7. Simplified symbol for operational amplifier.

The non-inverting input has a positive sign, as there is no phase inversion at this input. Similarly, the inverting input has a negative sign, due to the phase inversion that occurs at this terminal.

The output voltage is given by the formula in equation (2.2), and from this equation, we obtain:

$$V_d = \frac{V_o}{G} \tag{2.4}$$

This equation is particularly useful because sometimes it is extremely easy to measure the output voltage, which is not the case with the input voltage. In this scenario, V_o is measured to calculate V_d.

In general, the most important data that the user of an amplifier should remember are the input impedance, voltage gain, and output impedance. Figure 2.8 shows the equivalent circuit of an operational amplifier.

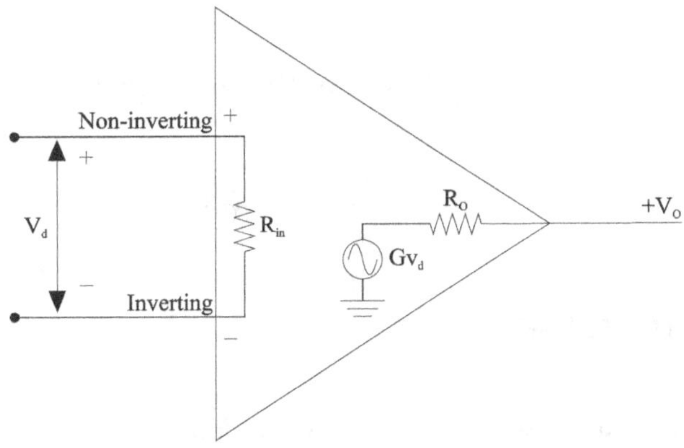

Figure 2 8. Equivalent circuit of an operational amplifier.

EXAMPLE 2.5

A 741 C has an input voltage of 1μV. Determine the output voltage.

SOLUTION

We multiply the input voltage by the voltage gain. As mentioned earlier (See section 2.1), a 741C has a voltage gain of 100000. The output voltage is:

$$V_o = 100000(1\mu V) = 0.1V$$

This response assumes that there is no load resistance connected to the operational amplifier.

If there were a load resistance, part of the voltage would drop across the output impedance of the amplifier.

EXAMPLE 2.6

A 741C has an output voltage of 5V. Determine the input voltage if the voltage gain is 100,000.

SOLUTION

We divide the output voltage by the voltage gain.

$$V_d = \frac{5V}{100000} = 50\mu V$$

Tension Offset

When both input terminals of an operational amplifier are connected to ground, a small voltage appears at the output (which can reach up to 2V in some references), which can result in significant errors when applications require handling small-value signals. (Figure 2.9)

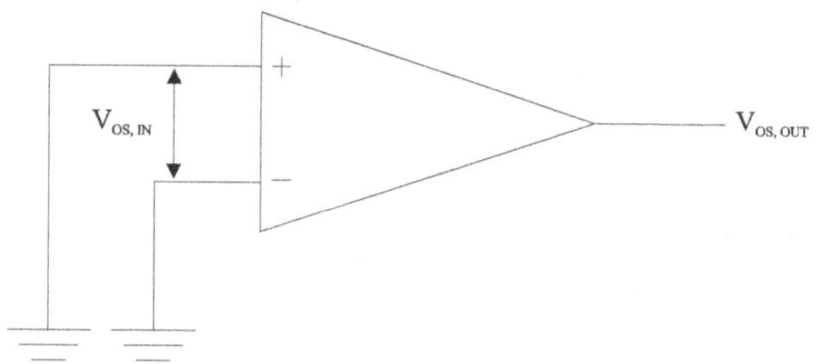

Figure 2-9. Output offset voltage.

This output voltage, called output offset voltage, is due to the input transistors having different values of V_{BE}. For example, in the datasheets of the 741C, typical values indicate an input offset voltage of ±2mV. This 2mV difference is an undesired signal because it gets amplified and produces an offset voltage at the output.

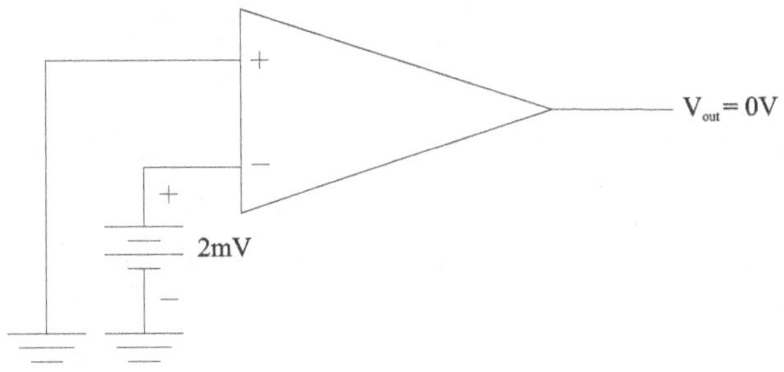

Figure 2-10. Output offset voltage compensation.

One way to eliminate this voltage is by applying a 2mV voltage at the inverting input, as shown in Figure 2.10. This way, the output offset voltage will be reduced to zero. However, since the offset voltage can have any polarity, it may sometimes be necessary to change the polarity of the 2mV.

EXAMPLE 2.7

An operational amplifier 741C has an input offset voltage of 2mV. Determine the output offset voltage without feedback.

SOLUTION

The input offset voltage is:

$$V_{os,\ in} = 2mV$$

The output offset voltage can be calculated as:

$$V_{os,\ sal} = GV_{os,\ in}$$

For a 741C, it was mentioned that the gain G is 100000. Then:

$$V_{os,\ sal} = 100000(2)(10^{-3}) = 200V$$

This is a high value and occurs when the signal is measured without feedback resistance, i.e., in open loop. When there is feedback resistance, the value of the output offset voltage is much lower, as we will see.

Advantages of feedback in offset compensation

Feedback involves applying (feeding back) a portion of the output voltage to the input of the operational amplifier.

It is called negative feedback when the feedback signal is applied to the inverting input of the Op-Amp, and positive feedback when the feedback signal is applied to the non-inverting input of the Op-Amp. This feedback has an improving effect on almost everything: it stabilizes the voltage gain, increases the input impedance, decreases the output impedance, reduces distortion, and output offset voltage.

Figure 2.11 shows a feedback amplifier with an output offset voltage in series with the original input voltage, V_{in}. The actual output offset voltage is much smaller for this circuit due to negative feedback.

The reason is that a portion of the output offset voltage is fed back to the inverting input, creating an effect equivalent to placing a voltage compensation source at the same terminal.

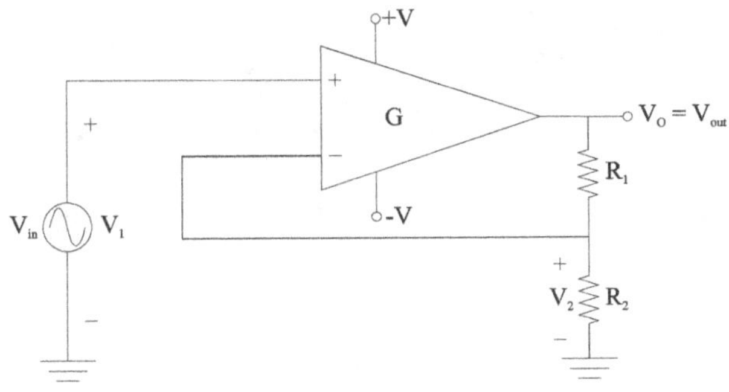

Figure 2-11. Negative feedback operational amplifier.

If necessary, the output offset voltage in closed loop can be reduced through three procedures:

The first one consists of reducing the closed-loop voltage gain to 100 by varying the feedback resistors.

The second option is to replace the operational amplifier with a better one. Some amplifiers, like the LM11C, have an input offset voltage of 0.1mV, resulting in a lower output offset voltage as well.

The third alternative is described in the datasheets of an Op-Amp 741C. It involves connecting a 10KΩ potentiometer between its terminals 1 and 5, with the wiper connected to the negative power supply, as shown in Figure 2.12. By adjusting the potentiometer, the offset voltage can be nullified.

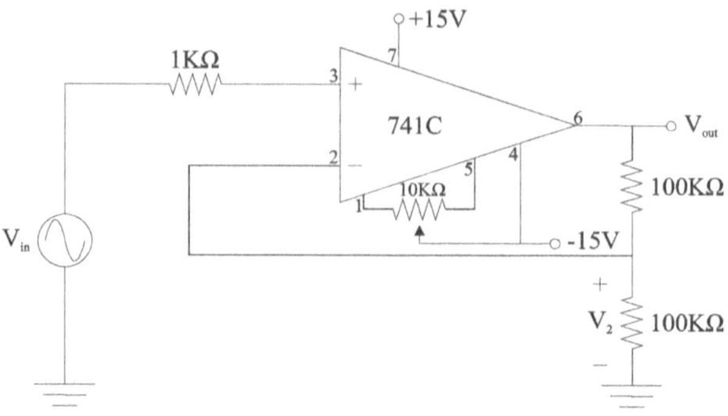

Figure 2-12. Circuit for output offset voltage compensation.

Negative feedback

Figure 2.12 shows an Op-Amp with external resistor connections. It can be observed that the output voltage is displayed through a voltage divider. As a result, a voltage is fed back to the inverting input of the operational amplifier. The value of this voltage can be calculated as follows:

$$V_2 = \frac{V_o}{R_1 + R_2} R_2 \tag{2.5}$$

The values of R_1 and R_2 determine the voltage at the inverting input, which can vary between 0 and V_o. In this type of amplifier with negative feedback, the input voltage is applied to the non-inverting terminal of the operational amplifier. Thus:

$$V_i = V_{in}$$

Also, remember that we had defined the differential voltage as:

$$V_d = V_1 - V_2$$

The operational amplifier amplifies this voltage, as mentioned earlier, resulting in:

$$V_o = GV_d$$

EXAMPLE 2.8

In the circuit of Figure 2.13, the voltage V_1 is 2mV and the voltage V_2 is 1mV. Calculate the differential voltage and the output voltage.

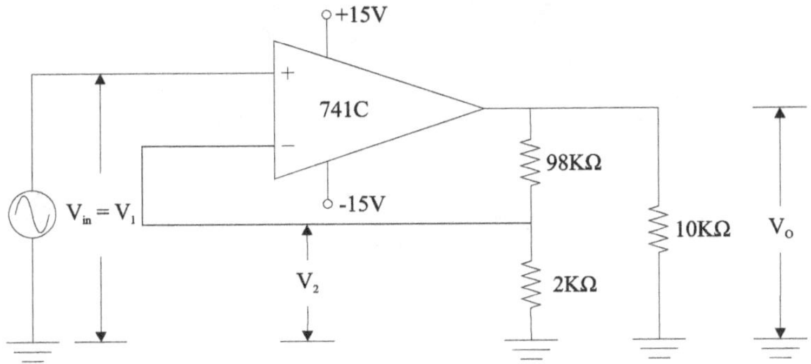

Figure 2-13. Circuit of example 2.8.

SOLUTION

The differential voltage is given by:

$$V_d = V_1 - V_2 = 2mV - 1mV = 1mV$$

From equation (2.5), it follows that:

$$V_o = \frac{R_1 + R_2}{R_2} V_2$$

Replacing with $R_1 = 98K\Omega$ and $R_2 = 2K\Omega$.

The gain will be:

$$G = \frac{V_o}{V_d} = \frac{50mV}{1mV} = 50$$

Ideal voltage gain

In expression (2.5), sometimes the fraction $\frac{V_2}{V_o}$ is denoted as B, reducing the expression to:

$$V_2 = BV_o \tag{2.6}$$

Where:

$$B = \frac{R_2}{R_1 + R_2} \tag{2.7}$$

As seen before:

$$V_d = V_1 - V_2$$

This differential voltage is amplified, resulting in an output voltage of approximately.

$$\frac{V_o}{V_{in}} = \frac{G}{1 + GB} \tag{2.8}$$

This formula shows the effect of negative feedback on the amplifier. It can be seen that the voltage gain with negative feedback is lower than the differential voltage gain of the operational amplifier. The quotient B is fundamental in the effect of negative feedback. When B is small, the negative feedback is small, and the voltage gain approaches G. But when it is large, the negative feedback is large, and the voltage gain is much lower than G. The product GB is called the "loop gain" because it represents the voltage gain that is achieved when traversing the entire circuit, from input to output and back to the input.

When the loop gain GB is much greater than 1, equation (2.8) reduces to:

$$\frac{V_o}{V_{in}} = \frac{1}{B} \tag{2.9}$$

This equation tells us that the voltage gain is equal to the inverse of B, the feedback fraction.

Remember that for equation (2.9) to hold, GB must be much greater than 1.

EXAMPLE 2.9

If the 741C in Figure 2.13 has a differential voltage gain of 100,000, what is the voltage gain of the operational amplifier?

SOLUTION

The fraction B, given by the voltage divider, has a feedback of:

$$B = \frac{2K\Omega}{98K\Omega + 2K\Omega} = 0.02$$

The loop gain is:

$$GB = 100000(0.02) = 2000$$

As this is much greater than 1, 1/B can be used as an approximation of the voltage gain:

$$\frac{V_o}{V_{in}} = \frac{1}{B} = \frac{1}{0.02} = 50$$

The exact response can be calculated as:

$$\frac{V_o}{V_{in}} = \frac{G}{1 + GB} = \frac{100000}{1 + 100000(0.2)}$$

In other words:

$$\frac{V_o}{V_{in}} = 49.975$$

Which is a value quite close to 50.

Open-loop and closed-loop voltage gain

The open-loop voltage gain, G_{LA}, is defined as the ratio V_o/V_{in}, with the feedback path open, as seen in Figure 2.14. To prevent the terminal impedances from being altered, the input inverting terminal is grounded through an equivalent resistance of:

$$R_3 = \frac{R_1 R_2}{R_1 + R_2} \tag{2.10}$$

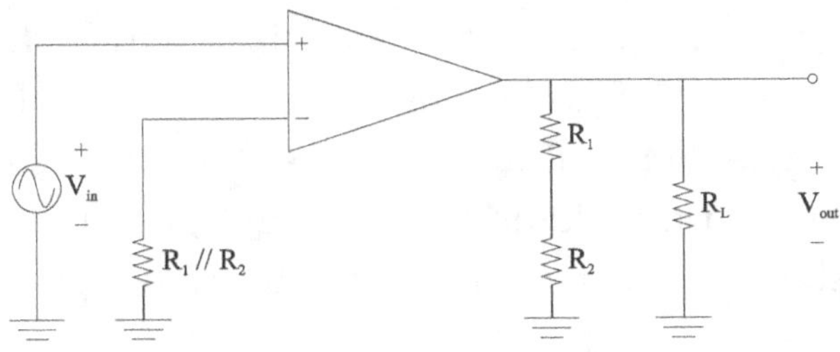

Figure 2-14. Open loop connection.

In a 741C, the open-loop voltage gain is generally 100,000. The closed-loop voltage gain corresponds to the circuit when feedback is closed, and it is denoted as G_{LC}. It is calculated as:

$$G_{LC} = \frac{G_{LA}}{1 + G_{LA}B} = \frac{V_o}{V_{in}}$$

In most feedback amplifier circuits, the loop gain $G_{LA}B$ is much greater than 1, so the previous equation reduces to:

$$G_{LC} = \frac{1}{B}$$

Since $B = R_2/(R_1 + R_2)$, an alternative form of the expression is:

$$G_{LC} = \frac{R_1 + R_2}{R_2}$$

Which can be written as:

$$G_{LC} = 1 + \frac{R_1}{R_2}$$

The voltage gain in closed loop is identical to V_{sal}/V_{in} studied in the previous section. Likewise, the voltage gain in open loop is identical to the differential voltage gain G. It is important to understand both concepts, as they appear in the datasheets and technical specifications provided by manufacturers.

It is important to remember and consider that, without negative feedback, the operational amplifier saturates immediately, as the input offset voltage multiplied by the open-loop gain drives the output stage into saturation. Monolithic operational amplifiers are designed to be used with some form of feedback. Without it, they have an excessively high voltage gain, making them unsuitable for most applications.

REVIEW

Concepts

Define or discuss the following:

- Operational Amplifier (op-amp).
- Terminals of an operational amplifier in an integrated circuit (IC).
- Saturation voltage.
- Open-loop voltage gain.
- Closed-loop voltage gain.
- Input offset voltage.
- Output offset voltage.
- Positive feedback.
- Negative feedback.
- Offset voltage compensation.

EXERCISES

Note: Where necessary, assume the values you find appropriate.

2.1.   An operational amplifier is subjected to an input signal of 0.2mV. If it has a differential gain of 100000, calculate the magnitude of the output signal.

2.2.   For the previous exercise, calculate the gain in decibels.

2.3.   In the output terminal of a 741C, a measurement of 10V is obtained. Calculate the magnitude of the applied input signal.

2.4. An operational amplifier has a gain of 100dB. If a voltage of 1mV is applied to its inverting terminal and a voltage of 2mV to its non-inverting terminal, determine the voltage value at the output.

2.5. The two input terminals of an operational amplifier are connected to ground, and at the output, an offset voltage of 0.5mV is measured. Determine the input offset voltage if the gain is 90dB.

2.6. An operational amplifier 741C is powered by a dual power supply of ±12V. Determine the saturation voltage and the maximum voltage that should be applied to the input terminals to achieve these saturation voltages.

2.7. A voltage of 1mV is applied to the inverting input of an operational amplifier, and a voltage of -1mV is applied to the non-inverting input. Calculate the output voltage obtained if the gain of the operational amplifier is 100000.

2.8. The two inputs (inverting and non-inverting) of an operational amplifier are connected to ground through two 220KΩ resistors. If a voltage of 0.8V is measured at the output, determine the differential voltage between the two input transistors of the operational amplifier.

2.9. Calculate, in decibels, the gain of an operational amplifier that has an output voltage of 5V when a 10mV input is applied.

2.10. Given the circuit shown in Figure 2.14, calculate B. If the gain with respect to the differential voltage is 100,000, calculate the gain with respect to the input voltage, V_{in}. The output is 2V.

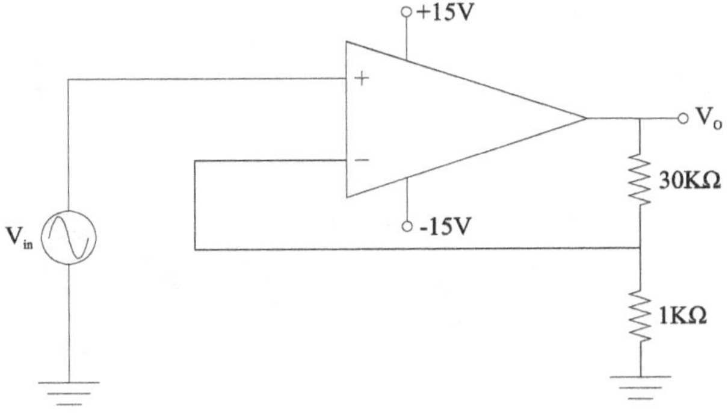

Figure 2-15. Circuit of exercise 2.10.

Chapter 3
OPERATIONAL AMPLIFIER
APPLICATIONS

In this chapter, different application circuits using operational amplifiers will be discussed. These circuits should be operated under normal conditions of the Op-Amp, that is, avoiding its saturation.

Non voltage inverting amplifier

A non-inverting voltage amplifier is shown in Figure 3.1. A signal applied to its non-inverting input terminal will appear at the output, amplified with the same phase.

The output voltage will be given by the expression:

$$V_o = \left(1 + \frac{R_f}{R_1}\right) V_i \tag{3.1}$$

The expression $\left(1 + R_f/R_1\right)$ represents the voltage gain due to negative feedback.

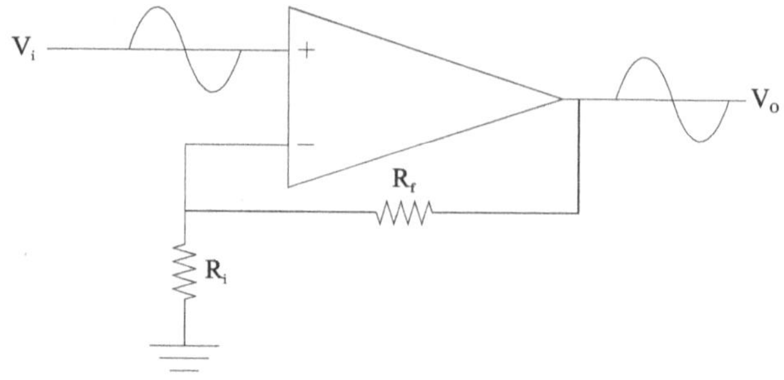

Figure 3-1. Non-inverting amplifier.

EXAMPLE 3.1

Calculate the output voltage of a non-inverting amplifier (like the one in Figure 3.1), given $V_i = 2V$, $R_f = 500K\Omega$, and $R_1 = 100K\Omega$.

SOLUTION

Using equation (3.1), we obtain:

$$V_o = \left(1 + \frac{R_f}{R_1}\right) V_i = \left(1 + \frac{500K\Omega}{100K\Omega}\right) 2V = 6(2V)$$

That is:

$$V_o = 12V$$

Voltage inverting amplifier

Figure 3.2 shows an inverting voltage amplifier circuit. The input signal is applied to the terminal marked with (-), and the output shows an amplified signal with a phase inverted compared to the input signal. The terminal marked with (+)

is directly connected to ground. The output voltage is given by the expression:

$$V_o = \frac{R_f}{R_1} V_i \qquad (3.2)$$

Where the expression $(- R_f/R_i)$ corresponds to the voltage gain. The negative sign in the expression indicates the phase inversion of the output signal relative to the input signal.

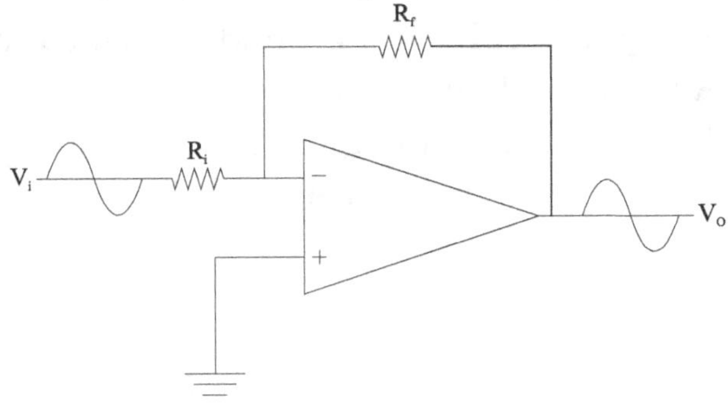

Figure 3-2. Voltage inverting amplifier.

EXAMPLE 3.2

The circuit in Figure 3.2 has $R_1 = 100K\Omega$ and $R_f = 500K\Omega$. Determine the output voltage if the input $V_i = -2V$.

SOLUTION

If we use equation (3.2), we obtain:

$$V_o = \frac{R_f}{R_1} V_i = -\frac{500K\Omega}{100K\Omega}(-2V) = -5(-2V)$$

That is:

$$V_o = 10V$$

Note that the sign of the output signal is positive, while the sign of the input signal is negative. This difference is precisely what accounts for the phase inversion that occurs in this circuit.

Physical earth and virtual earth

The inverting input of an operational amplifier is a virtual ground. Unlike a physical ground, which has a voltage of 0V and an extremely high current (theoretically infinite), the virtual ground has a voltage of 0V and a current of 0A. Thus, the circuit in Figure 3.2 can be redrawn as shown in Figure 3.3.

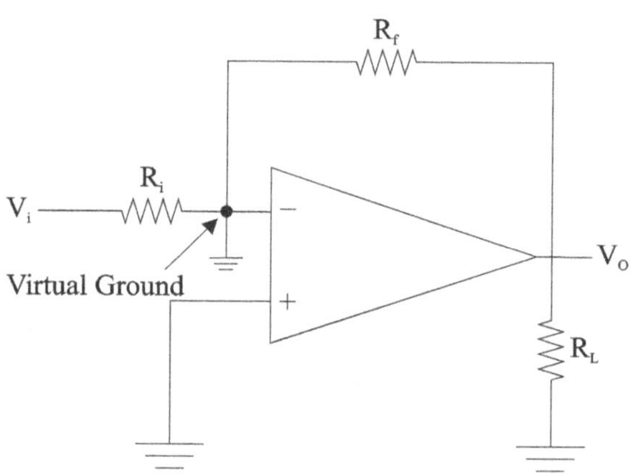

Figure 3-3. Virtual ground in an operational amplifier.

Note in the circuit how the input voltage V_i and the input resistance R_1 form a closed loop due to the virtual ground at the inverting terminal. Similarly, the feedback resistor R_f

is in parallel with the output resistance R_L. With these considerations, anyone interested in the derivation of equations (3.1) and (3.2) will have made noteworthy progress.

EXAMPLE 3.3

Use the circuit in Figure 3.3 to determine the voltage gain formula (consider the concept of virtual ground).

SOLUTION

The input circuit of the operational amplifier, with the virtual ground appearing at the inverting terminal, is shown in Figure 3.3 (a).

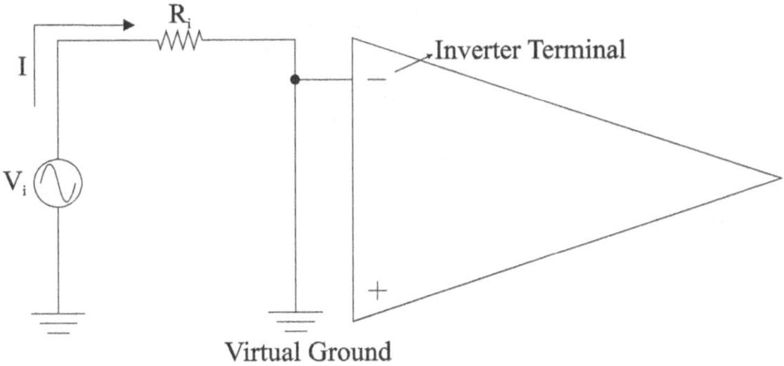

Figure 3-3 (a) Input circuit of the inverting operational amplifier in Figure 3.3.

The current I can be calculated as follows:

$$I = \frac{V_i}{R_1}$$

Similarly, a circuit for the output of the operational amplifier is shown in Figure 3.3 (b).

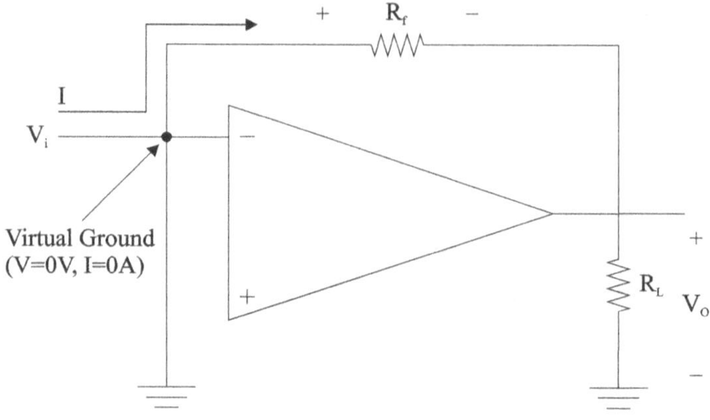

Figure 3-3 (b) Output circuit of the inverting operational amplifier of figure 3.3.

Since the resistor R_f and the resistor R_L are in parallel, their voltages are equal, and therefore:

$$IR_f = -V_o$$

Alternatively:

$$I = -\frac{V_o}{R_f}$$

Combining the two equations that relate to the same current I, we obtain:

$$\frac{V_o}{V_i} = -\frac{R_f}{R_1}$$

Which is identical to equation (3.2).

Unit follower

In Figure 3.4, the circuit of a unity follower can be seen. This circuit provides a gain of 1 without phase inversion. In this circuit, considering the virtual ground at the inverting terminal, it is clear that the output voltage is equal to the input voltage. That is:

$$V_o = V_i \tag{3.3}$$

This implies, in addition to the fact that the polarity of the input signal is the same as the polarity of the output signal, that the magnitudes of the signals are identical.

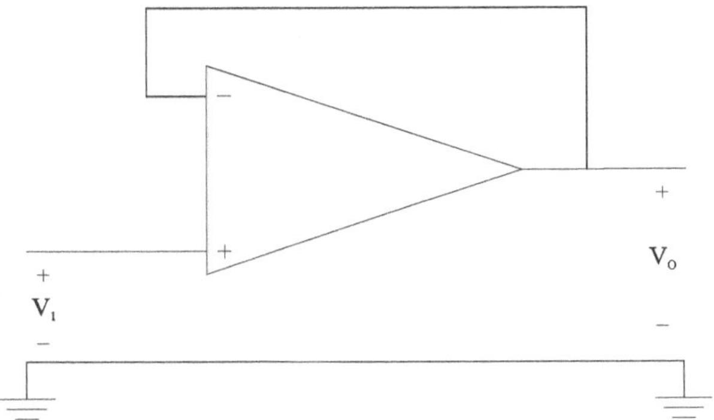

Figure 3-4. Unit follower.

Comparators

Sometimes it is necessary to compare two signals and determine which one is greater and which one is smaller. For this purpose, operational amplifier comparators are used, with a reference signal applied to one terminal and the signal to be compared applied to the other terminal. These circuits are also known as voltage level detectors and can be either inverting or non-inverting, as will be seen below.

Positive level detectors

In Figure 3.5, a positive reference voltage, V_{ref}, is applied to one of the terminals of the Op-Amp. This means that the Op-Amp is enabled as a comparator to detect a positive voltage. If the voltage to be detected, V_i, is applied to the positive terminal of the operational amplifier, the result is a non-inverting positive-level detector. Its operation is shown by the waveforms in Figure 3.5(a). When V_i is above V_{ref}, then V_o is equal to $+V_{sat}$. When V_i is below V_{ref}, V_o is equal to $-V_{sat}$.

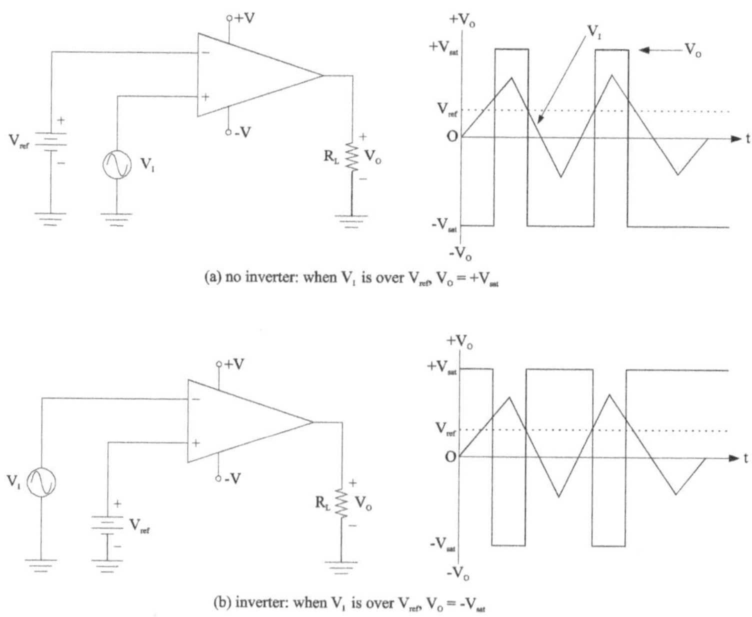

Figure 3-5. Positive voltage level detector (a) non-inverting (b) inverting.

If V_i is applied to the inverting input, as shown in Figure 3.5(b), the circuit becomes an inverting positive-level detector. Its operation is as follows: when V_i is above V_{ref}, V_o is equal to $-V_{sat}$; and when V_i is below V_{ref}, V_o is equal to $+V_{sat}$. This circuit's action can be seen more clearly in Figure 3.5(b), where V_i and V_{ref} are compared over time.

EXAMPLE 3.4

In the circuit of Figure 3.5(a), the supply voltage +V and -V is ±15V. If the reference voltage, $V_{ref} = 5V$, and the input voltage, $V_i = 10V$.

Explain the operation of the circuit and place the different values on the signals.

SOLUTION

From the previous explanation, we know that the circuit corresponds to a positive-level detector. Similarly, in section 2.2, the concept of saturation voltage was explained, so we now know that if the bias voltage is ±15V, the saturation voltage will be ±13V. The signal $V_i = 10V$ will be compared to the reference voltage, $V_{ref} = 5V$. When the voltage V_i is greater than the reference voltage, the output signal will be $+V_{sat}$, and when the voltage V_i is less than the reference voltage, the output voltage will be $-V_{sat}$. For this case, the diagram with the input, reference, and output signals will be as shown in Figure 3.6.

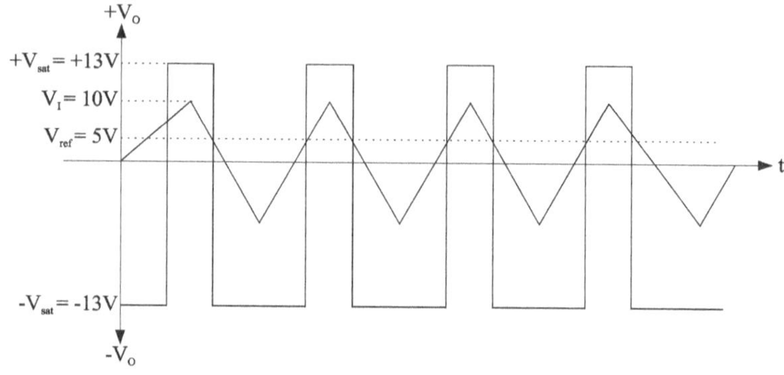

Figure 3-6. Example 3.4 circuit waveforms.

Negative level detectors

Figure 3.7(a) is a non-inverting negative-level detector. This circuit detects when the input signal V_i crosses the negative voltage $-V_{ref}$. When V_i is above $-V_{ref}$, V_o is equal to $+V_{sat}$. When V_i is below $-V_{ref}$, $V_o = -V_{sat}$.

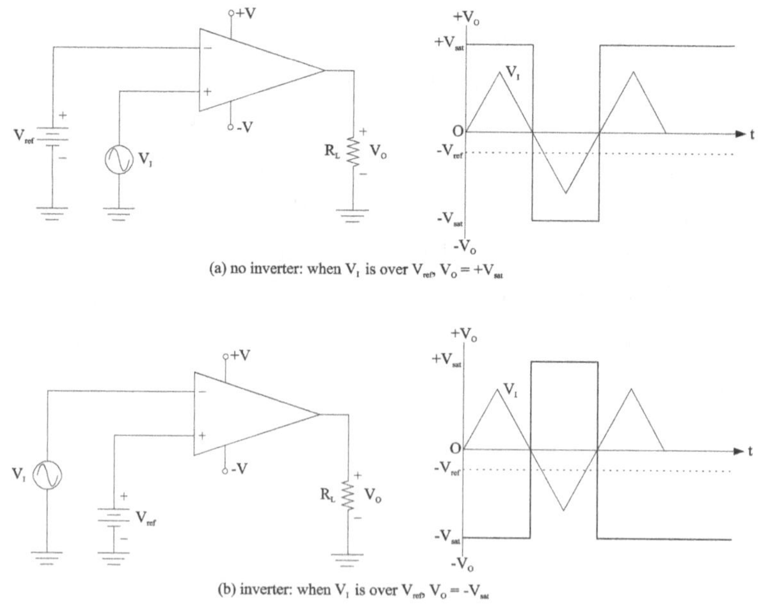

Figure 3-7. Negative voltage level detector, (a) non-inverting (b) inverting.

The circuit in Figure 3.7 (b) is an inverting negative-level detector. When V_i is above $-V_{ref}$, V_o is equal to $-V_{sat}$, and when V_i is below $-V_{ref}$, V_o is equal to $+V_{sat}$.

Sine to square wave converter

The particular case where V_{ref} is equal to zero in both types of level detectors seen in the previous section leads us to a sine-to-square wave converter.

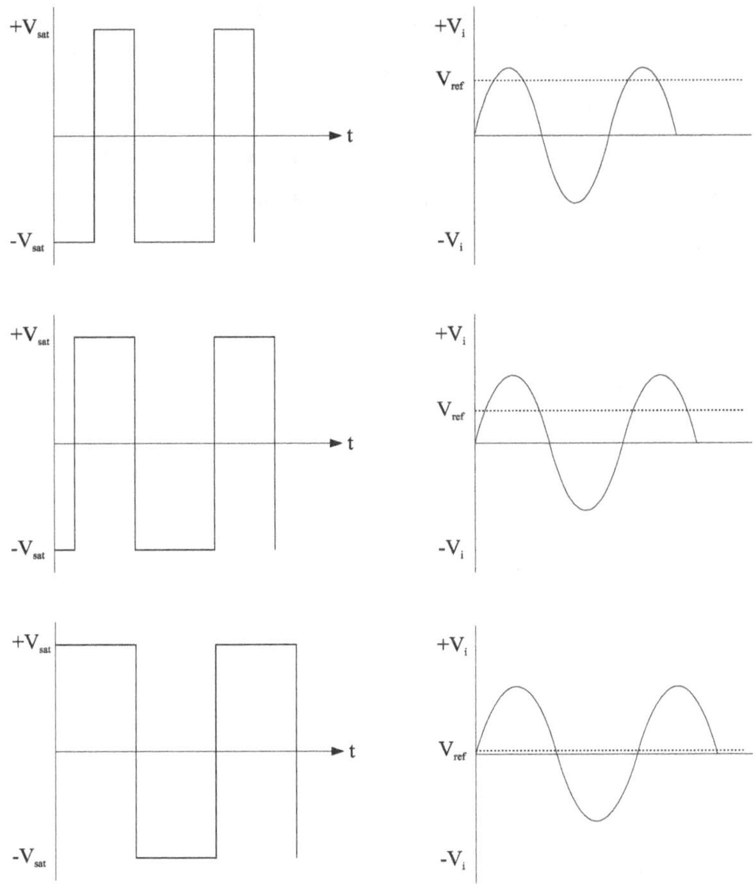

Figure 3-8. Pulse width modulation by varying reference voltage level.

In the previous cases, it can be observed that the width of the positive and negative pulses in the output signal depends on the magnitude of V_{ref}. If the reference voltage is remarkably close to the maximum value of the input voltage, the output signal will have wide positive (or negative) half-cycles and narrow negative (or positive) half-cycles. As V_{ref} approaches zero, the widths of the half-cycles become more equal. If V_{ref} becomes zero (coinciding with the horizontal axis of the Cartesian plane), the output signal will be completely symmetric, resulting in a square wave from a sinusoidal or triangular wave (Figure 3.8).

EXAMPLE 3.5

Given the circuit in Figure 3.9, explain its behavior and draw the waveforms it produces, along with their respective values.

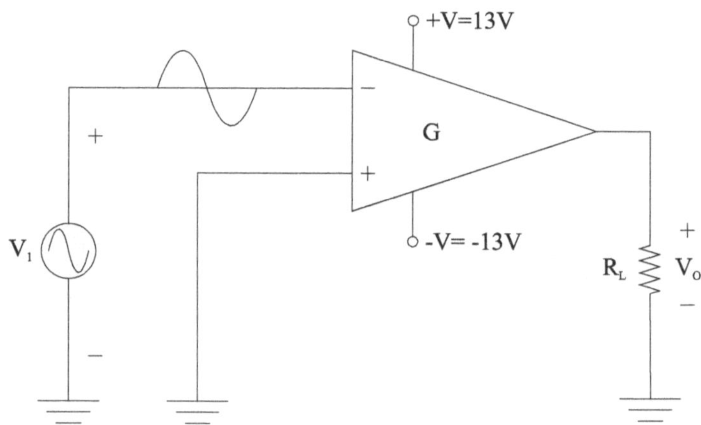

Figure 3-9. Example circuit 3.5.

SOLUTION

With the circuit arrangement shown, without feedback resistance, the Op-Amp is operating as a comparator. Since a sinusoidal signal is applied to the inverting terminal and the inverting terminal is connected to ground, the circuit functions as an inverting positive-level detector. The reference voltage coincides with the zero axis of the Cartesian plane, so the output signal will be as shown in Figure 3.10, with $\pm V_{sat} = \pm 11V$; that is, the output voltage will be $V_o = \pm 11V$.

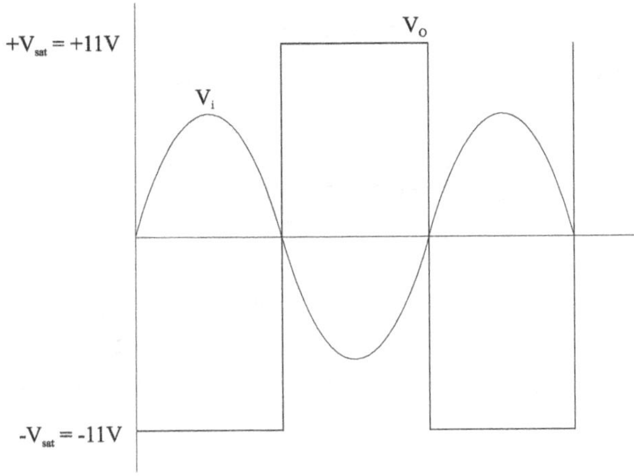

Figure 3-10. Input and output signals of the circuit of example 3.5.

The summing amplifier

One of the most useful Op-Amp circuits used in analog computers is the summing amplifier circuit. Figure 3.11 shows a three-input summing circuit, which provides a means of algebraically adding three input voltages, each multiplied by a constant gain factor.

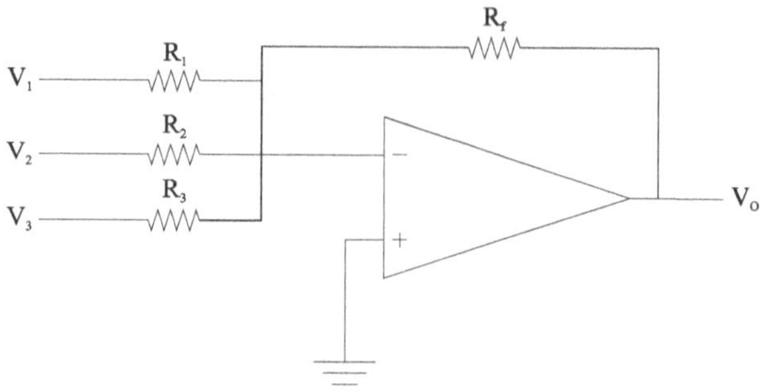

Figure 3-11. Adder amplifier.

The output voltage can be determined in terms of the inputs as follows:

$$V_o = -\left(\frac{R_f}{R_1}V_1 + \frac{R_f}{R_2}V_2 + \frac{R_f}{R_3}V_3\right) \qquad (3.4)$$

In simple terms, each input adds a voltage to the output, as obtained from a constant gain inverting circuit. If more inputs are used, they add additional components to the output.

EXAMPLE 3.6

Determine the output voltage of the summing amplifier in Figure 3.11 for the following set of input voltages and resistances ($R_f = 1M\Omega$ in all cases).

(a) $V_1 = +1V$ $R_1 = 500K\Omega$
                $V_2 = +2V$ $R_2 = 1M\Omega$
                $V_3 = +3V$ $R_3 = 1M\Omega$

(b) $V_1 = -2V$ $R_1 = 200K\Omega$
                $V_2 = +3V$ $R_2 = 500K\Omega$
                $V_3 = +1V$ $R_3 = 1M\Omega$

SOLUTION

Using equation (3.4):

$$V_o = -\left[\frac{1000K\Omega}{500K\Omega}(+1) + \frac{1000K\Omega}{1000K\Omega}(+2) + \frac{1000K\Omega}{1000K\Omega}(+3)\right]$$

$$V_o = -[2(+1) + 1(+2) + 1(+3)]$$

$$V_o = -7V$$

$$V_o = -\left[\frac{1000K\Omega}{200K\Omega}(-2) + \frac{1000K\Omega}{500K\Omega}(+3) + \frac{1M\Omega}{1M\Omega}(+1)\right]$$

$$V_o = -[5(-2) + 2(+3) + 1(+1)]$$

$$V_o = -[-10 + 6 + 1]$$

$$V_o = +3V$$

EXAMPLE 3.7

For the circuit in Figure 3.12, determine the output voltage.

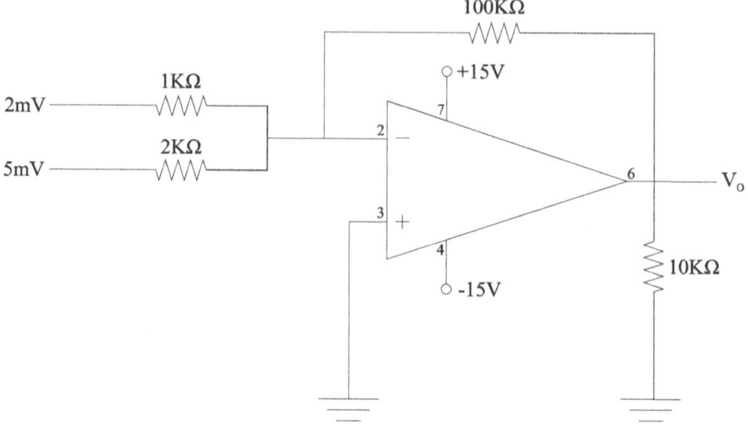

Figure 3-12. Circuit of example 3.7.

SOLUTION

Using equation (3.4).

$$V_o = -\left[\frac{100K\Omega}{1K\Omega}(2mV) + \frac{100K\Omega}{2K\Omega(5mV)}\right]$$

$$V_o = -[100(2mV) + 50(5mV)]$$

$$V_o = -450mV$$

In any case, the minus sign accounts for the output inversion with respect to the input voltage; in this example, the phase of the signal resulting from the algebraic sum of the different input signals.

The integrator

As its name implies, an integrator is a circuit that performs the mathematical operation of integration. The most popular application of an integrator is to generate a triangular or voltage ramp signal, which linearly increases or decreases the voltage. The basic circuit is shown in figure 3.13 (a).

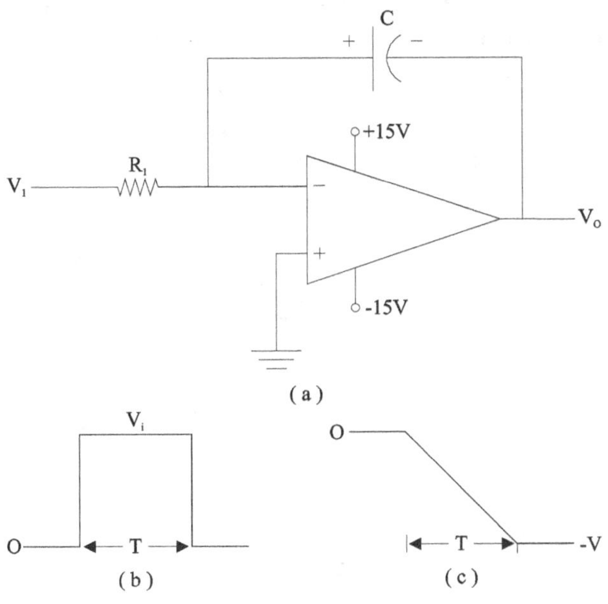

Figure 3-13. (a) Integrator circuit (b) Rectangular input (c) Characteristic output ramp.

For the signal to be a ramp, it is necessary for the input voltage to be a rectangular pulse, as shown in figure 3.13 (b). Figure 3.13 (c) shows the shape of the ramp signal obtained at the output.

The way to prove that the output voltage is a ramp is as follows: the basic law of the capacitor states that:

$$C = \frac{Q}{V}$$

Alternatively:

$$V = \frac{Q}{C} \tag{3.5}$$

Due to the high input resistance in the amplifier, the current given by $I = V_i/R_1$, which is a constant value, will flow through the capacitor, and therefore its charge Q will increase linearly with respect to time. This results in the capacitor having a voltage in the form of a negative ramp, as shown in Figure 3.13 (c). Dividing equation (3.5) by T, we have:

$$\frac{V}{T} = \frac{Q/T}{C}$$

And since the current through the load is constant, we can write:

$$\frac{V}{T} = \frac{I}{C}$$

Alternatively:

$$V = \frac{IT}{C} \tag{3.6}$$

This is the voltage across the capacitor at the end of the pulse.

EXAMPLE 3.8

In figure 3.14, calculate the voltage across the capacitor at the end of the pulse.

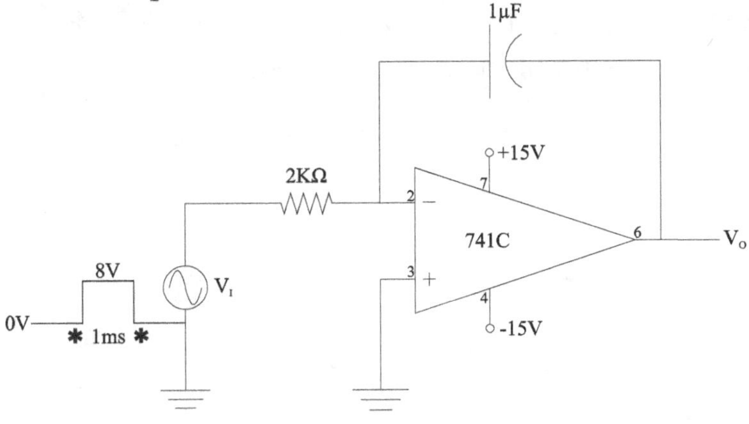

Figure 3-14. Circuit of example 3.8.

SOLUTION

Due to the virtual ground at the inverting input, the current through the input is:

$$I = \frac{8V}{2K\Omega} = 4mA$$

With equation (3.6), the output voltage at the end of the pulse will be:

$$V = \frac{(4mA)(1ms)}{1\mu F} = 4V$$

What emerges from the integrator, then, is a voltage that starts at 0V and decreases linearly to -4V. The waveform is similar to that shown in Figure 3.13 (c).

Multiple inputs can be applied to an integrator, as shown in Figure 3.15. The circuit arranged in this way is a summing integrator, as used in analog computers. The behavior is the same as in the case of a single input, except that the capacitor's charge will depend on the resulting current from the algebraic sum of the different inputs.

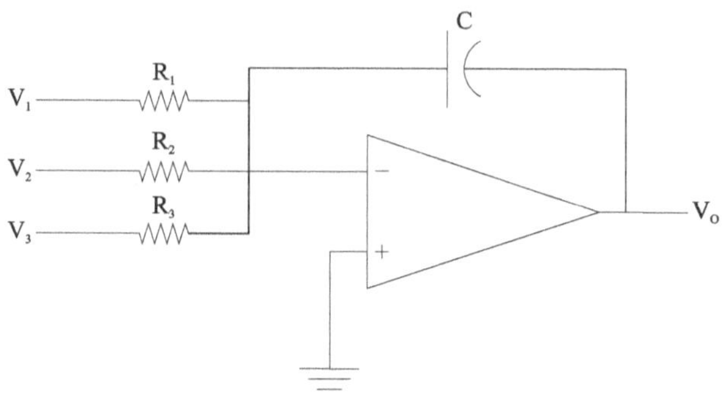

Figure 3-15. Amplifier as integrating adder.

The differentiator

A differentiator is a circuit that performs a mathematical operation called differentiation. Differentiation is the opposite operation to integration, which is performed by an integrator, as seen in the previous section. The differentiator produces an output voltage proportional to the rate of change of the input voltage with respect to time. Common applications of a differentiator include detecting the rising and falling edges of a rectangular pulse or generating a rectangular output from a ramp input.

Figure 3.16 shows a differentiator designed with an operational amplifier. You can notice the similarity with the previously seen integrator. The difference between them lies in the interchange of the capacitor and the resistor.

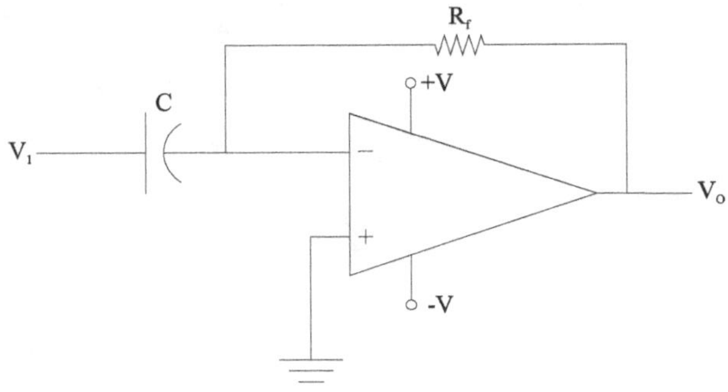

Figure 3-16. Differentiating Circuit.

A commonly used input with a differentiator is a ramp, as seen at the top of Figure 3.17. Due to the virtual ground, the entire input voltage appears across the capacitor. The voltage ramp implies that the current is constant, as shown in equation (3.7), which is deduced from equation (3.6).

$$I = \frac{CV}{T} \tag{3.7}$$

Given this current, the output voltage is given by:

$$V_o = IR_f \tag{3.8}$$

In an oscilloscope, you can observe the waveforms provided by all these circuits. For example, the rising edge of a rectangular pulse will appear perfectly vertical. But if the sweep time is shortened enough, you will see that the rising edge is generally an increasing exponential wave, which can be approximated to a positive ramp.

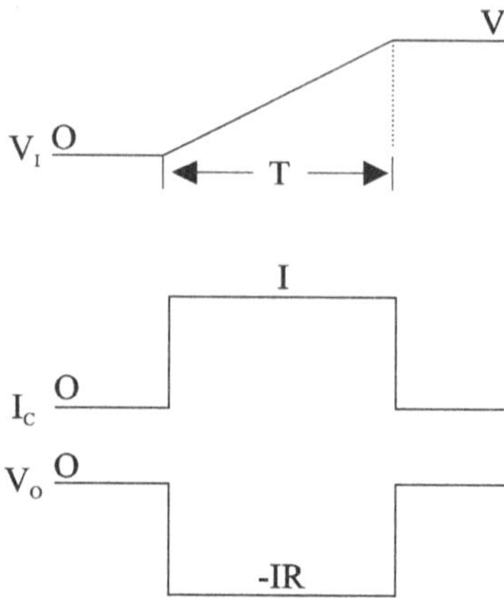

Figure 3-17. Inlet ramp produces a rectangular outlet.

Thus, a common application of the differentiator is the generation of voltage spikes like the ones shown in Figure 3.18.

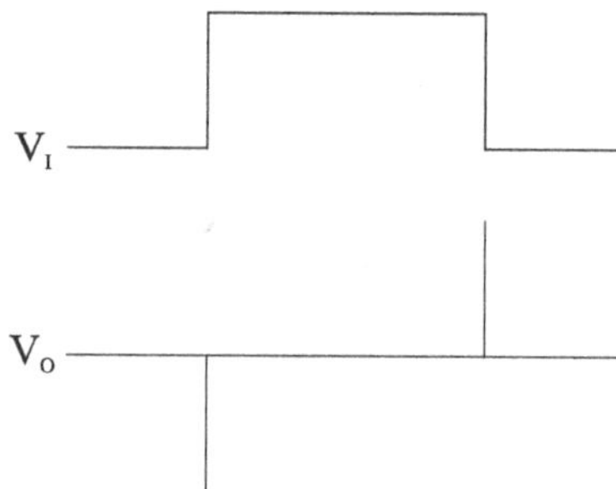

Figure 3-18. Rectangular input produces narrow voltage peaks at output.

The rising edge of the pulse is approximately a positive ramp, so the output will be a noticeably short negative voltage spike. Similarly, the falling edge of the input pulse is approximately a negative ramp, resulting in a narrow positive voltage spike at the output.

Sometimes it is customary to place a resistor in series with the capacitor to avoid the oscillations that are common in this differentiator circuit. A typical value for this resistor is between $0.01R_f$ and $0.1R_f$. With this added resistor, the closed-loop voltage gain is between 10 and 100. Its effect is to limit the closed-loop voltage gain at high frequencies, where the oscillation problem arises (Figure 3.19).

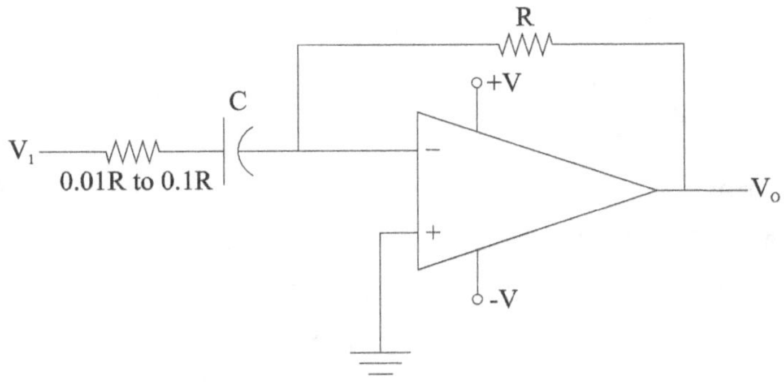

Figure 3-19. Resistor in series with capacitor avoids high frequency oscillations.

Logarithmic amplifier

Logarithms are a tool that facilitates mathematical operations such as multiplication, division, exponentiation, and root extraction. With logarithms, multiplication is reduced to addition and division to subtraction; exponentiation becomes multiplication, and root extraction becomes division. The final result is obtained by taking the antilogarithm of these operations. Figure 3.20 shows the circuitry of a basic logarithmic amplifier.

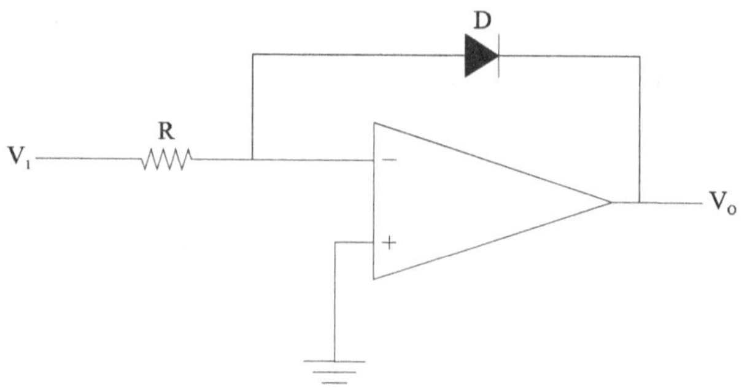

Figure 3-20. Logarithmic amplifier.

The main element of the logarithmic amplifier in Figure 3.20 is the diode D in the feedback loop. A diode has an inherent exponential characteristic, and therefore a logarithmic characteristic. The current through the diode, I_D, is given by:[1]

$$I_D = I_S\left(e^{qV_D/KT} - 1\right) \tag{3.9}$$

Where:

I_S: Reverse saturation current

e: Base of natural logarithms

$(e = 2.718)$

V_D: Voltage of the diode

q: Electron charge, $1.6(\llbracket 10 \rrbracket^{-9})C$

K: Boltzmann constant

---

[1] For a better understanding of obtaining these formulas, advanced electronics books should be consulted.

$$\left(K = \frac{1.38(10^3)J}{K}\right)$$

T: Temperature, K (in Kelvin)

At room temperature, equation (3.9) reduces to:

$$I_D = I_S e^{39V_D} \tag{3.10}$$

The output-input relationship for the logarithmic amplifier in figure 3.20 would be then:

$$V_o = (-26mV)\left(L_n\left(\frac{V_i}{R}\right) - L_n(I_s)\right) \tag{3.11}$$

EXAMPLE 3.9

Calculate the output voltage, V_o, of the basic logarithmic amplifier in figure 3.20, for an input voltage of 3V. The resistor $R = 10K\Omega$ and the reverse saturation current, I_s, for the diode is 10nA.

SOLUTION

By substituting these values into equation (3.11), we obtain:

$$V_o = (-26mV)\left[L_n\left(\frac{3}{10^4}\right) - L_n\left(10(10^{-9})\right)\right]$$

$$V_o = -749.6mV$$

Anti-logarithmic amplifier

To complete the mathematical operations involving logarithms, it is necessary to have a circuit that performs the opposite operation, namely, antilogarithm. The antilogarithm is used to express the logarithm as the corresponding number.

To obtain the antilogarithm of the logarithm of a number, you take the exponential of the logarithm.

$$e^{Ln(Z)} = Z$$

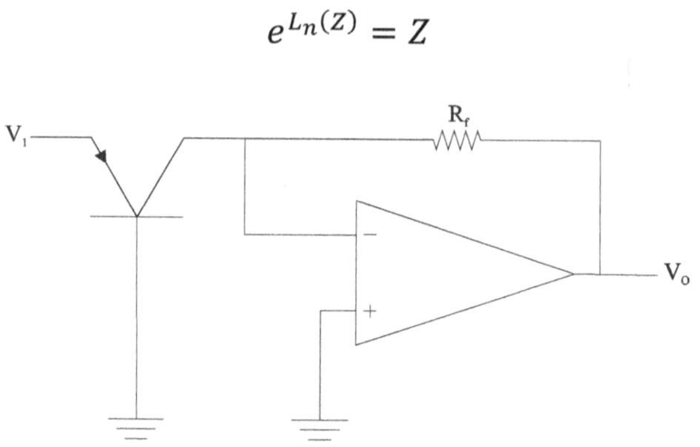

Figure 3-21. Anti-logarithmic amplifier.

Therefore, the antilogarithm function is basically the exponential function. A transistor placed at the input of the amplifier generates the antilogarithm function. The transistor configuration should be common base. An amplifier circuit serving as an antilogarithm function generator is shown in Figure 3.21.

Waveform converters

Operational amplifiers are also especially useful for converting sine waves into square waves, square waves into triangular waves, and so on. In the following, we will see some circuits that convert a waveform applied to the input into another waveform at the output.

Sinusoidal to rectangular wave converter

Figure 3.22 shows a Schmitt trigger, which produces a square wave output when any input signal is applied. For the output to occur, the input signal must be large enough to exceed the bias voltage. In this case, the output will have an oscillating signal, switching between $+V_{sat}$ and $-V_{sat}$. In figure 3.22 (a), the shape of the input signal can be seen at the top, and the output signal at the bottom.

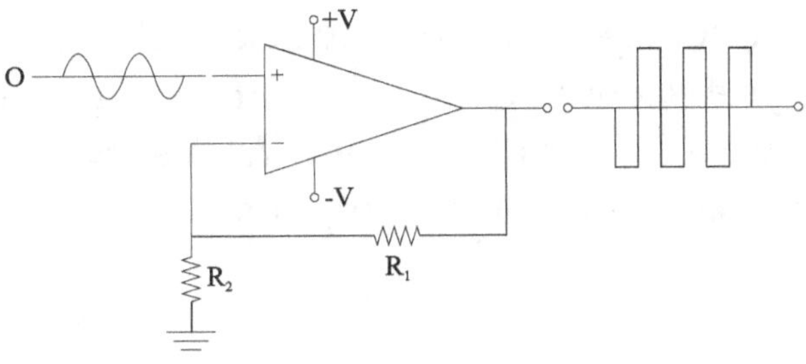

Figure 3-22. Schmitt scale.

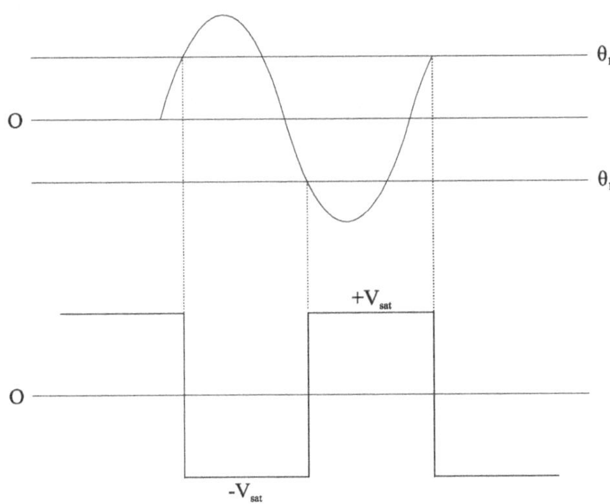

Figure 3-22 (a) Input - output signals.

The input waveform does not have to be sinusoidal, as shown in figures 3.22 and 3.22 (a). The signal can have any shape, as long as it is periodic and large enough to exceed the switching points, θ_1 and θ_2, determined by the amplifier's bias voltage. The frequency of the output signal will always be the same as that of the input signal.

Rectangular to triangular wave converter

Figure 3.23 (a) shows an integrator to which a rectangular input signal is applied. As can be seen in Figure 3.23 (b), the ramp has a negative slope during the positive half-cycle of the input voltage and a positive slope during the negative half-cycle. Consequently, the output signal will be a triangular waveform with the same frequency as the input signal. The magnitude of the output signal is given by the expression:

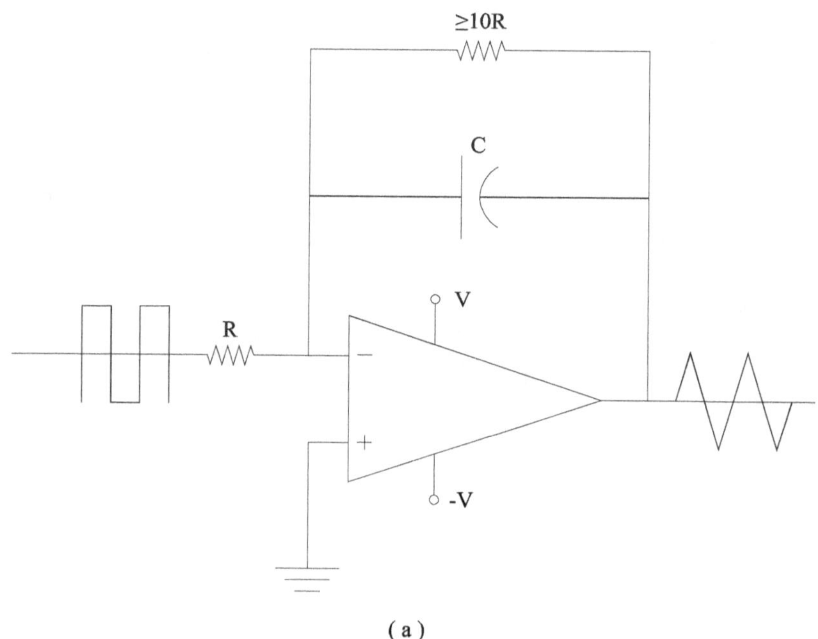

(a)

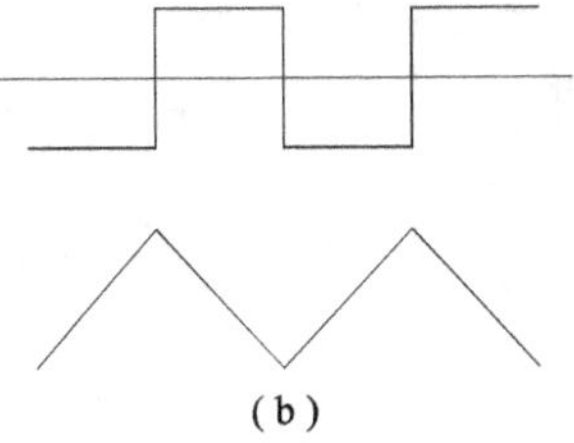

(b)

Figure 3-23 (a) Square signal applied to an integrator (b) Input - output signals.

$$V_o = \frac{V_i}{4fRC} \tag{3.12}$$

Where V_o and V_i are given in peak-to-peak values.

Triangle wave to pulse converter

In Figure 3.24 (a), a triangular input is applied to a comparator circuit, which converts it into a rectangular signal. By varying the resistance R_2, the width of the output pulses can be adjusted, which is equivalent to varying the duty cycle. In Figure 3.24 (b), W represents the pulse width, and T is the period. The duty cycle, D, is defined as the pulse width divided by the period.

$$D = \frac{W}{T}(100\%) \tag{3.13}$$

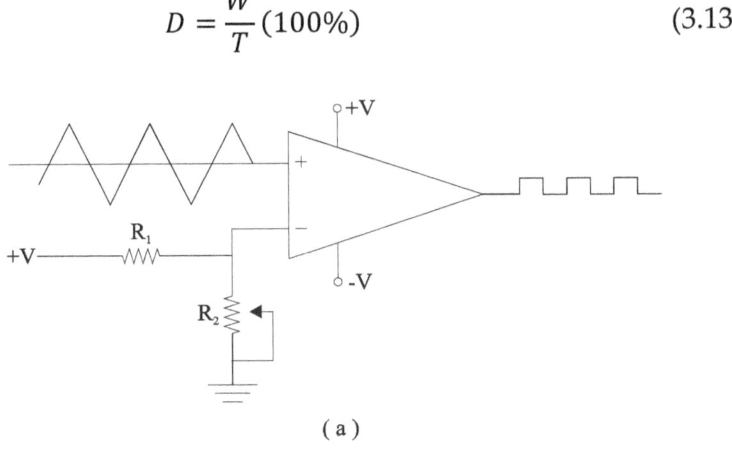

(a)

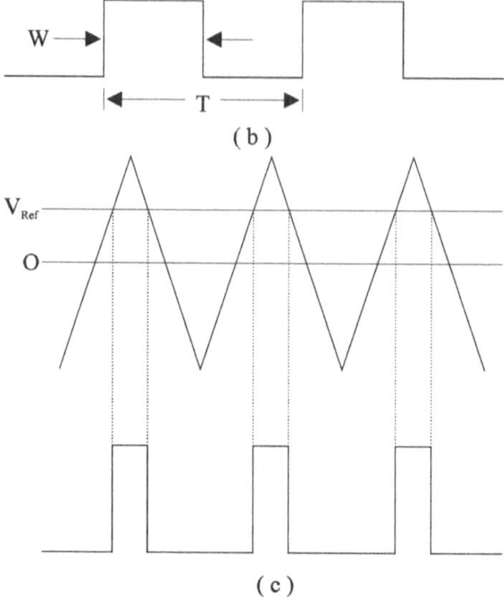

Figure 3- 24 (a) Comparator with triangular input. (b) Output with variable duty cycle. (c) Waveform at input and output.

EXAMPLE 3.10

A rectangular input is applied to the integrator in Figure 3.25. If the frequency is 1kHz and the peak-to-peak value is 10V, determine the output voltage.

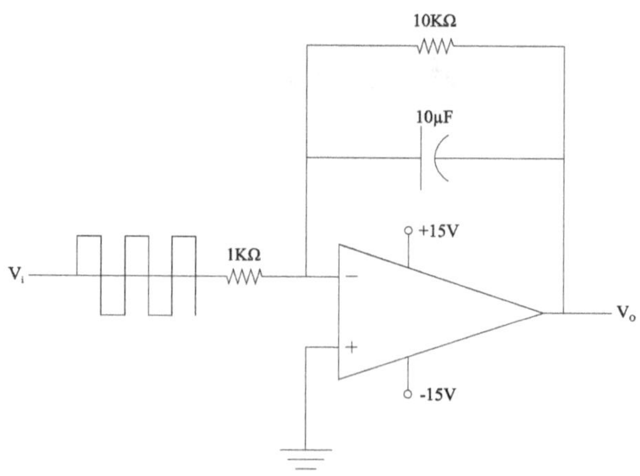

Figure 3-25. Circuit of example 3.10.

SOLUTION

From equation (3.12), the output is a triangular waveform with a peak-to-peak voltage of:

$$V_o = \frac{10V}{4(1KHz)(1K\Omega)(10\mu F)} = 0.25V$$

EXAMPLE 3.11

A triangular waveform is applied to the input of the circuit in Figure 3.26. If the frequency is 1kHz, determine the frequency of the output signal and the duty cycle when the potentiometer slider is at the midpoint of its range.

SOLUTION

Each output pulse occurs during the half-cycle of the input voltage. Therefore, the frequency of the output signal is identical to the frequency of the input signal, which is 1kHz.

When the potentiometer's cursor is at the midpoint of its value, 5KΩ, the reference voltage is:

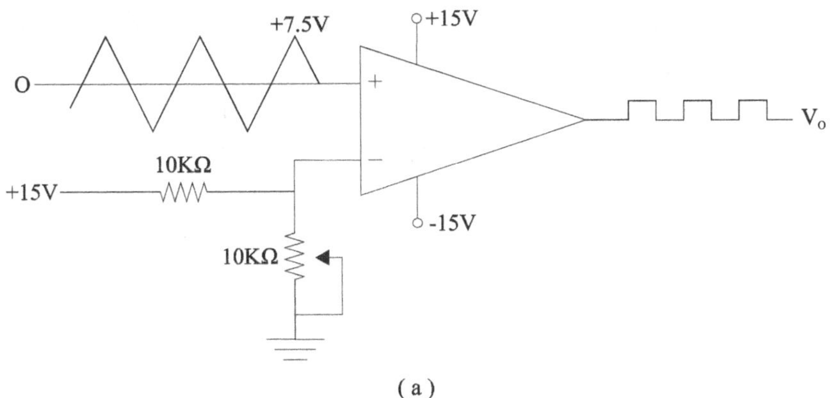

(a)

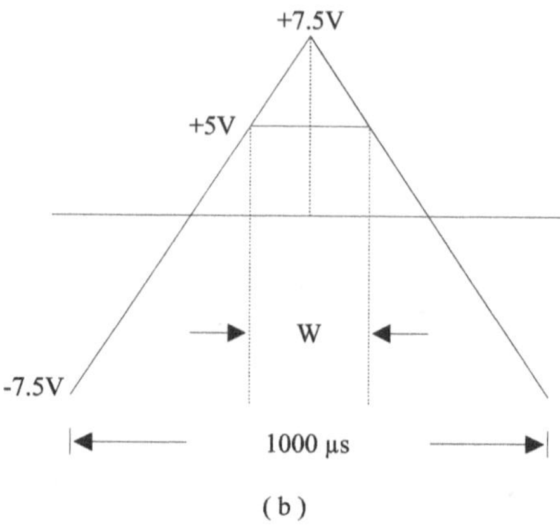

Figure 3-26. Circuit diagram and input waveform of example 3.11.

$$V_{ref} = \frac{15V\,(5K\Omega)}{15K\Omega} = 5V$$

The period of the input and output signals is:

$$T = \frac{1}{f} = \frac{1}{1KHz} = 1ms = 1000\mu s$$

In Figure 3.26 (b), this value is indicated as.

To make the input signal transition from -7.5V to +7.5V, 500µs are required.

The width of the output pulse is W. From the geometry of figure 3.26 (b), the following relationship can be established.

$$\frac{W/2}{500\mu s} = \frac{7.5V - 5V}{15V}$$

Solving for W, we have:

$$W = 167\mu s$$

And the duty cycle will be:

$$D = \frac{W}{T} = \frac{167\mu s}{1000\mu s}(100\%)$$

That is to say:

$$D = 16.7\%$$

REVIEW

Concepts

Define or discuss the following:

- Non-inverting voltage amplifier.
- Inverting voltage amplifier.
- Physical ground and virtual ground.
- Unity follower.
- Positive level detector.
- Negative level detector.
- Summing amplifier.
- Integrating amplifier.
- Differentiating amplifier.
- Logarithmic amplifier.
- Antilogarithmic amplifier.
- Sinewave to square wave converter.
- Rectangular wave to triangular wave converter.
- Triangular wave to pulse converter.
- Phase of a signal and phase shift of an output signal with respect to an input signal.
- Voltage gain of a unity follower.
- Reference voltage of a comparator.
- Output voltage of a comparator.
- Sinusoidal input waveform converter with $V_{ref} = 0$.
- Duty cycle of a pulse signal from a triangular wave.
- Closed-loop gain of an operational amplifier.

EXERCISES

3.1.   For the circuit in Figure 3.27, determine the output voltage. If in this same circuit $R_f = 1M\Omega$ and $R_1 = 10k\Omega$, what will be the value of the output voltage? What waveform will the output signal have? What will be the phase of the output signal?

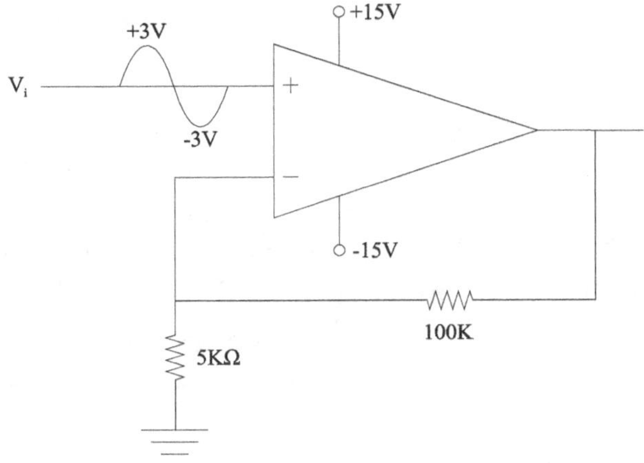

Figure 3-27. Circuit of exercise 3.1.

3.2.   The circuit given in figure 3.28 is an inverting voltage amplifier. If R_f can be varied using the switch, let us determine the magnitude of the three signals that can be obtained when connecting the switch in positions 1, 2, and 3.

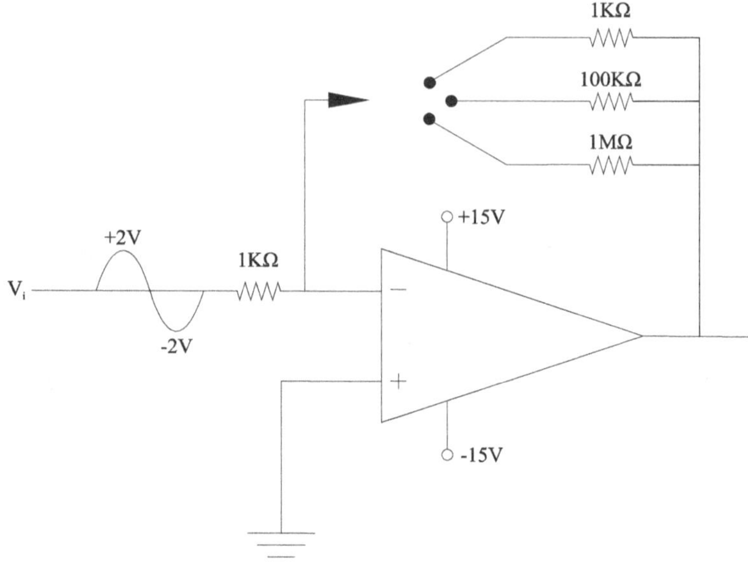

Figure 3-28. Circuit of exercise 3.2.

3.3. For the circuit in figure 3.29, let us determine the value of the input current and the voltage across the load resistor. The given parameters are: $V_i = 5V$, $R_1 = 100\Omega$, $R_L = 5K\Omega$, and $R_f = 5K\Omega$.

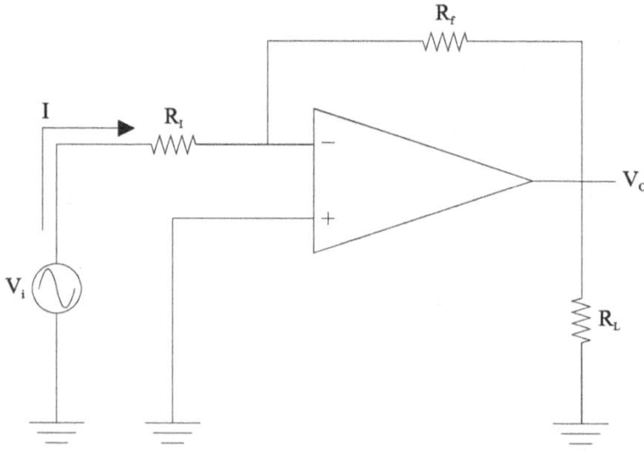

Figure 3-29. Circuit of exercise 3.3.

3.4.   Repeat the previous exercise with $V_i = 7mV$, $R_1 = 200\Omega$, $R_f = 10K\Omega$, and $R_L = 2K\Omega$.

3.5.   Use the concept of virtual ground to obtain an equivalent circuit of the circuit shown in Figure 3.30 and prove that the output voltage of a unity gain buffer is equal to the applied input voltage.

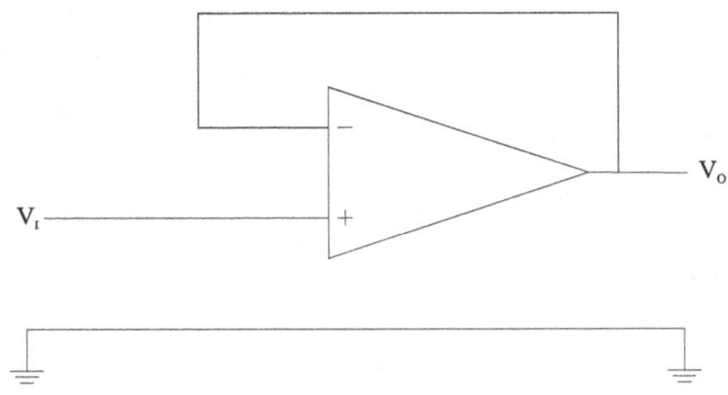

Figure 3-30. Circuit of exercise 3.5.

3.6.   Given the comparator shown in Figure 3.31, determine the value of the reference voltage.

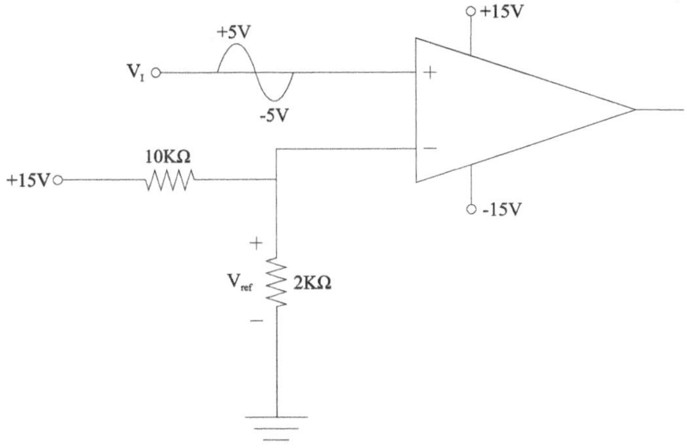

Figure 3-31. Circuit of exercise 3.6.

3.7.   For the circuit in Figure 3.31, obtain the output signal for the given conditions. Explain how the circuit operates.

3.8.   Given the circuit in Figure 3.32, explain its operation and determine the output voltage (magnitude and waveform).

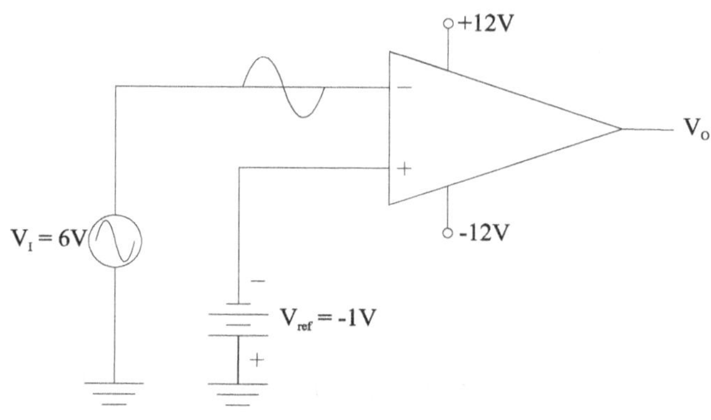

Figure 3-32. Circuit of exercise 3.8.

3.9.   Determine the waveform of the output signal of the circuit given in Figure 3.33.

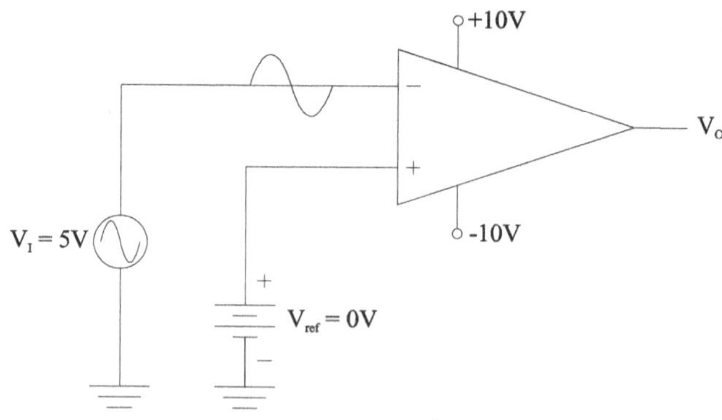

Figure 3-33. Circuit of exercise 3.9.

3.10. If the negative bias terminal of the operational amplifier given in Figure 3.33 is connected to ground, what would be the new waveform of the output signal?

3.11. Given the circuit in Figure 3.34, determine the magnitude and phase of the output signal.

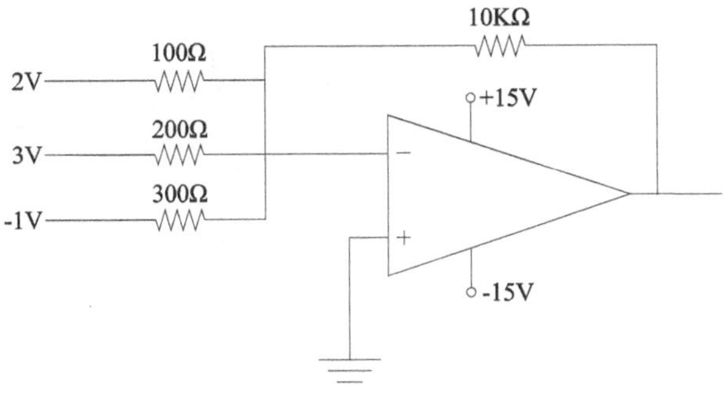

Figure 3-34. Circuit of exercise 3.11.

3.12. For the circuit in Figure 3.35, we have $R_1 = 1K\Omega$, $R_2 = 2K\Omega$, $R_3 = 3K\Omega$, $R_f = 100K\Omega$, the output voltage $V_o = 10V$, $V_i = 0.5V$, and $V_3 = 1.5V$. We need to calculate V_2.

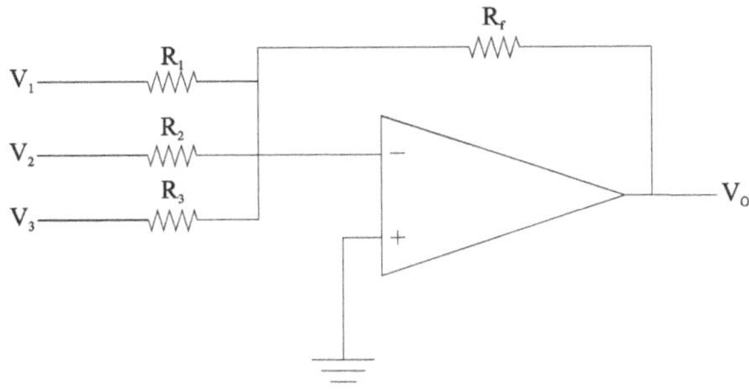

Figure 3-35. Circuit of exercise 3.12.

3.13. An integrator like the one shown in Figure 3.36 has an input voltage of 2V, $R_1 = 100\Omega$, and $C = 10\mu F$. If the period of the pulse applied to the input is 2ms, calculate the magnitude of the output voltage and draw the waveform of the signal.

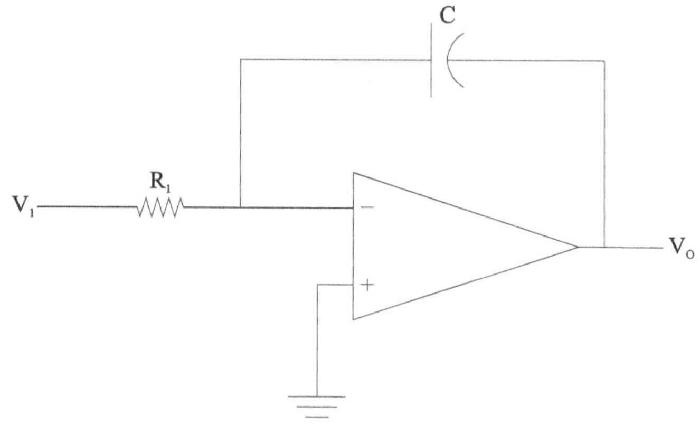

Figure 3-36. Circuit of exercise 3.13.

3.14. For the summing integrator shown in Figure 3.37, determine the magnitude of the output signal. The signals V_1, V_2, and V_3 are rectangular pulses with an amplitude of 3V, a period of 0.5ms, and the same phase.

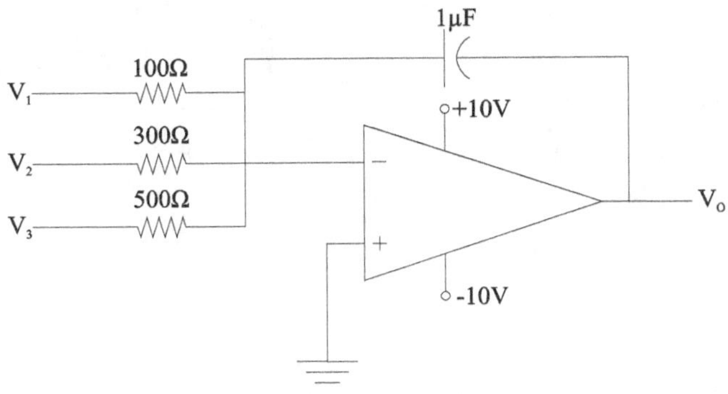

Figure 3-37. Circuit of exercise 3.14.

3.15. What would happen to the output signal of the circuit in Figure 3.36 if the applied input signal were a continuous (infinite period) signal?

3.16. In the circuit of Figure 3.36, the positions of the resistor and the capacitor are swapped. If the same signal as in exercise 3.13 is applied, what will be the output signal? What would happen to the waveform of the output if a 10ms period ramp with a positive peak value of 10V is applied to this same circuit?

3.17. In the previous exercise (differentiator circuit), a resistor is wanted to be placed in series with the capacitor to prevent any oscillations that may occur. What should be the value of this resistor?

3.18. Calculate the output voltage, V_o, of the logarithmic amplifier shown in Figure 3.38, assuming the diode's saturation current, I_s, is 8nA.

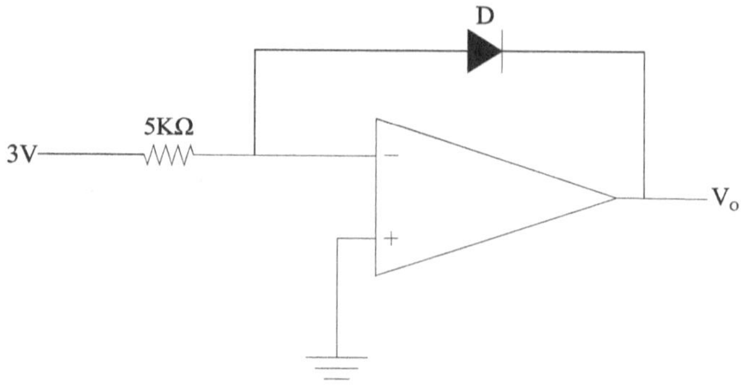

Figure 3-38. Circuit of exercise 3.18.

3.19.   Explain the operation of the circuit shown in figure 3.39.

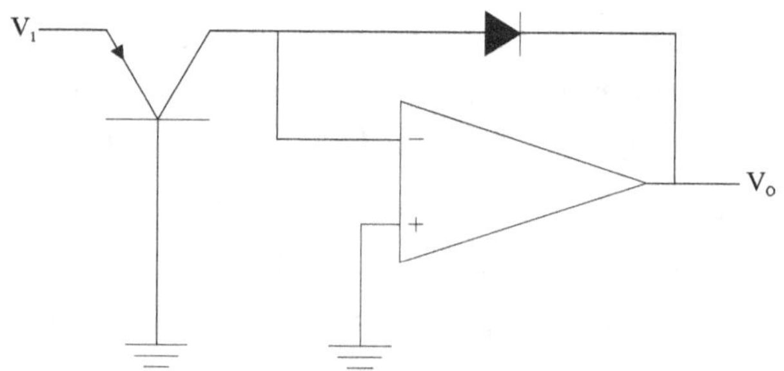

Figure 3-39. Circuit of exercise 3.19.

3.20.   For the circuit in figure 3.40, determine the reference voltage and the magnitude of the output pulses.

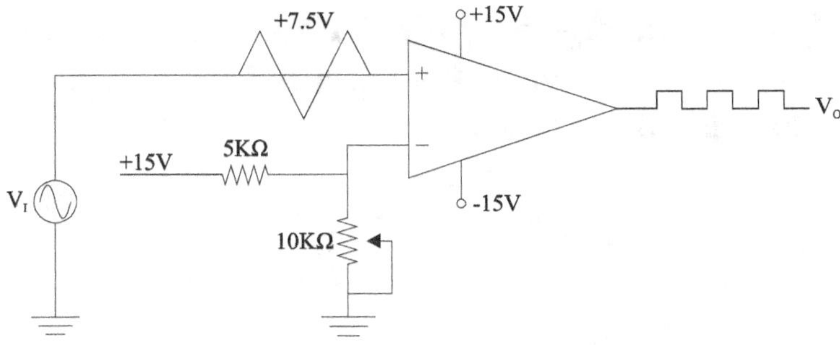

Figure 3-40. Circuit of exercise 3.20.

3.21. What is the duty cycle in the circuit of figure 3.40 when the cursor is at the top end and when it is at the bottom end?

3.22. The 741 in figure 3.41 has an open loop gain of 100,000. What is the closed-loop gain of the amplifier? Use an exact method and an approximate method to calculate it.

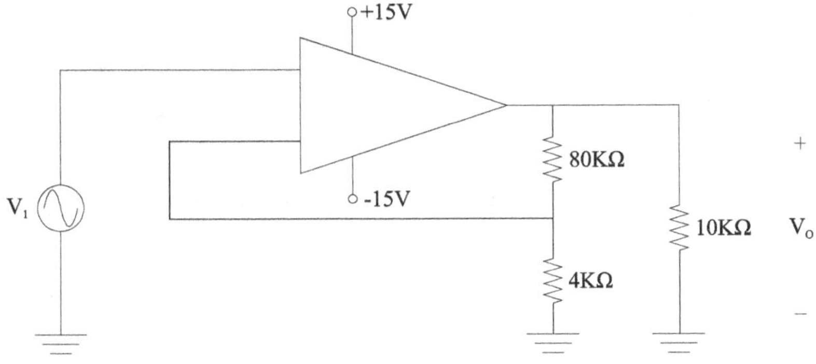

Figure 3-41. Circuit of exercise 3.22.

3.23. The operational amplifier in figure 3.42 produces an output of 1V when the input is 1mV. Calculate the gain in dB.

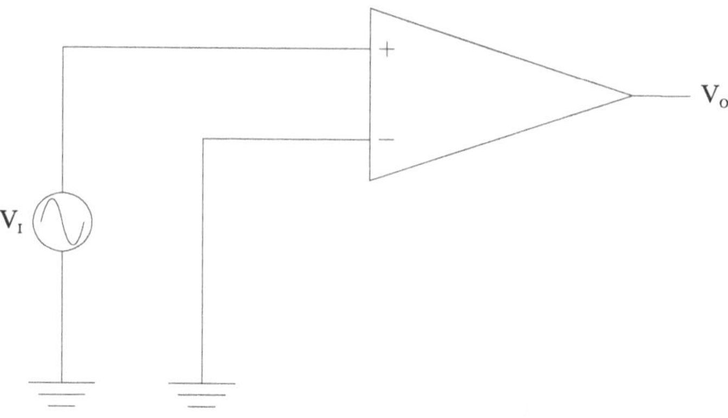

Figure 3-42. Circuit of exercise 3.23.

3.24. Draw the circuit of a non-inverting positive-level comparator.

3.25 What circuit (draw the schematic) can be used to generate edge-triggered signals for triggering an SCR?

3.26. You have 3 operational amplifiers connected in cascade (the input of the second one is the output of the first one, the input of the third one is the output of the second one). Determine a way to calculate the total gain of the system. Draw the circuit if the first amplifier is an inverter and the second and third amplifiers are non-inverters.

3.27. An inverting summing circuit has a feedback resistor of 100KΩ, and two inputs of 2mV and 5mV connected through resistors of 1KΩ and 2KΩ, respectively. If there is a 10KΩ resistor at the output, determine the output voltage and the current flowing through the load.

3.28. Calculate the gain of the amplifier system in figure 3.43.

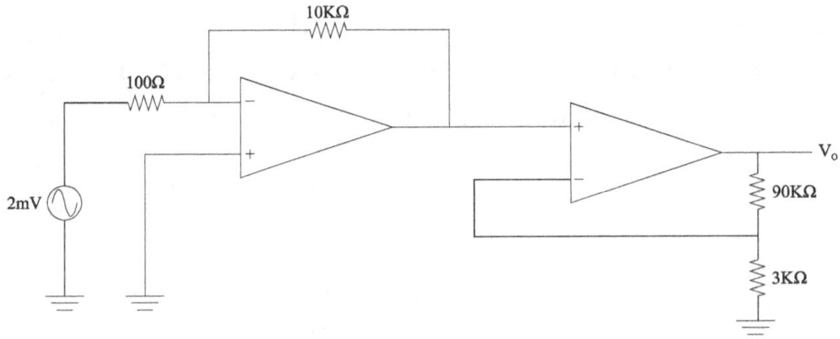

Figure 3-43. Circuit of exercise 3.28.

3.29. Calculate the output voltage of the circuit in figure 3.44.

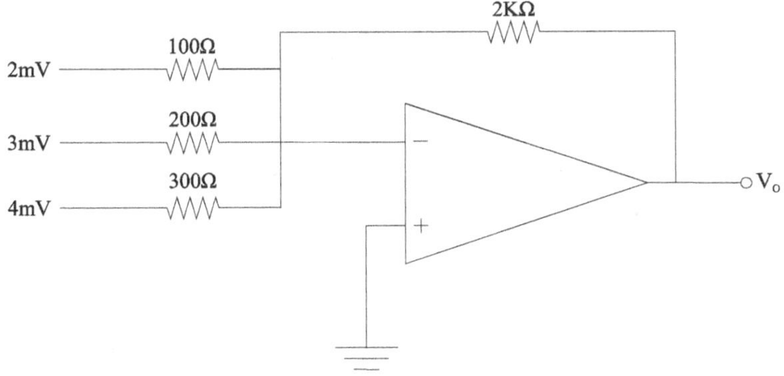

Figure 3-44. Circuit of exercise 3.29.

3.30. Draw the circuit of a generator that converts a sinusoidal waveform to a step waveform.

3.31. Draw a two-stage cascaded amplifier, with the first stage being an inverting amplifier and the second stage being a non-inverting amplifier.

3.32. In the circuit of Figure 3.45, determine the output voltage for the two extremes of the potentiometer (maximum and minimum).

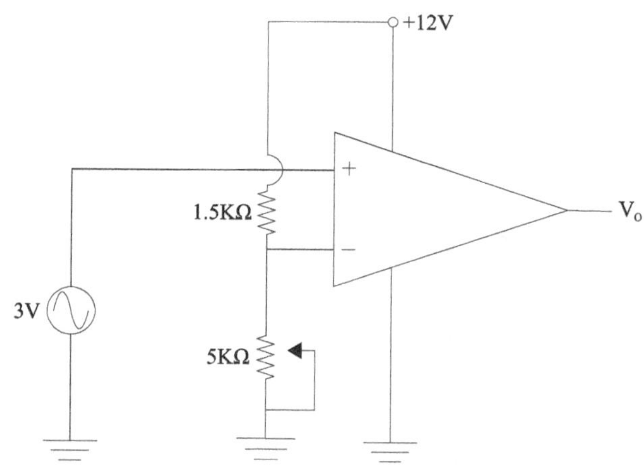

Figure 3-45. Circuit of exercise 3.32.

3.33. Think and explain what the output would be like in the circuit of Figure 3.46.

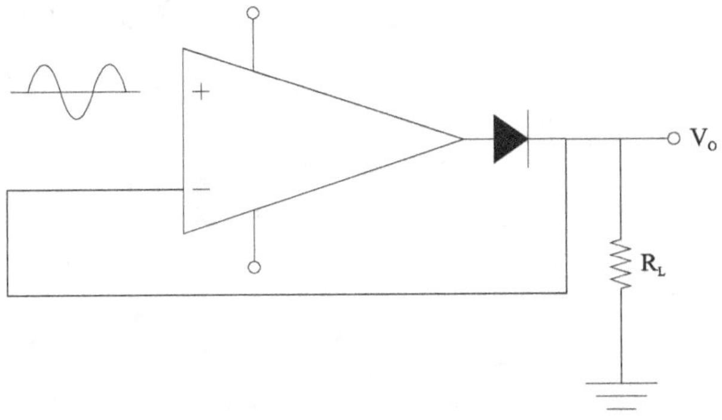

Figure 3-46. Circuit of exercise 3.33.

3.34. Draw comparator circuits (inverting or non-inverting), one for positive level and the other for negative level. Show how the voltage reference sources would be constructed using resistors and potentiometers.

3.35. Draw the circuit of a sine wave to square wave generator with an output voltage amplitude of 9V.

3.36. Draw the circuit of a ramp function generator with a signal period of 10ms. The input signal amplitude is 8mV and an output amplitude of 9mV is desired. Choose either the capacitor or the resistor and calculate the other parameter to ensure this operation.

3.37. For the circuit in Figure 3.47, determine the value of the output magnitude.

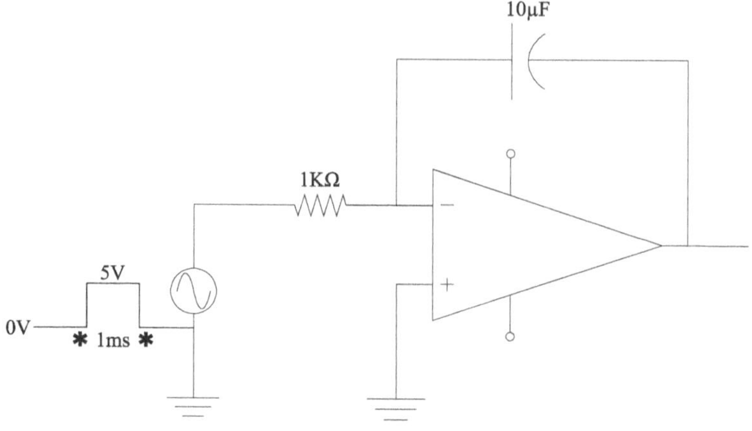

Figure 3-47. Circuit of exercise 3.37.

3.38. Calculate the gain of the circuit shown in Figure 3.48.

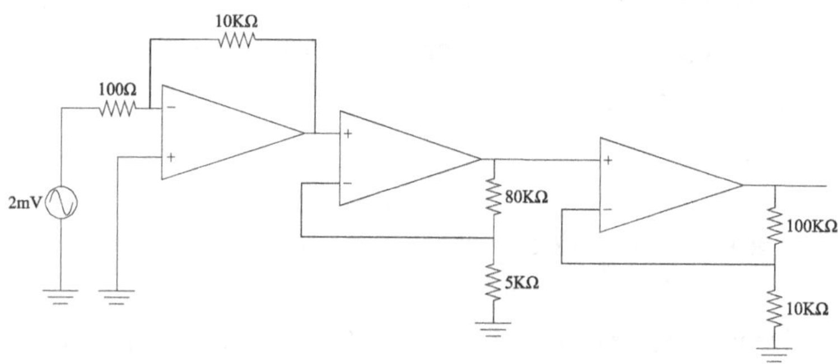

Figure 3-48. Circuit of exercise 3.38.

3.39. How could you generate a ramp signal from a sinusoidal signal? Explain and draw the circuit with the respective signals.

3.40. How could you generate short-duration pulse signals from a triangular signal? Explain and draw the circuit with the respective signals.

Chapter 4
SPECIAL DEVICES

When we talk about a special device in electronics, we are practically referring to all the elements that are available to the user in the technical market. Each element can be considered a product of the genius of human curiosity. Thanks to electronics and all its vast components, man has created this world of comforts, but also, it is due to it that the technical field requires more trained individuals, but even more so, specialized in a particular branch of science.

We can say that a special device is one that can fulfill a wide variety of purposes. Among these, there are quite a few, which we can name a few that we will see, such as the UJT (unijunction transistor), the 555 (timer IC), the SCR (silicon-controlled rectifier), the TRIAC, the DIAC, etc. All of great applicability and importance.

Unijunction Transistor (UJT)

As its name suggests, the unijunction transistor is a device that has only one junction.

Initially, the UJT (Unijunction Transistor) was called a double-base diode because its terminals are located at two different points, on each side of the junction, as shown in Figure 4.1 (a).

Another characteristic of the UJT is that it has a region of negative resistance. A device is said to have negative resistance when the voltage across the terminals of the device decreases for increasing currents.

The UJT, due to its negative resistance, is widely used in timing and triggering oscillator circuits for SCRs.

Figure 4.1 (b) shows the symbol of a UJT, and in Figure 4.1 (c), the equivalent circuit of the same device can be seen.

The resistor in the figure 4.1(a), known as the base bar resistor, R_{BB}, is typically in the range of 4000 to 12000Ω.

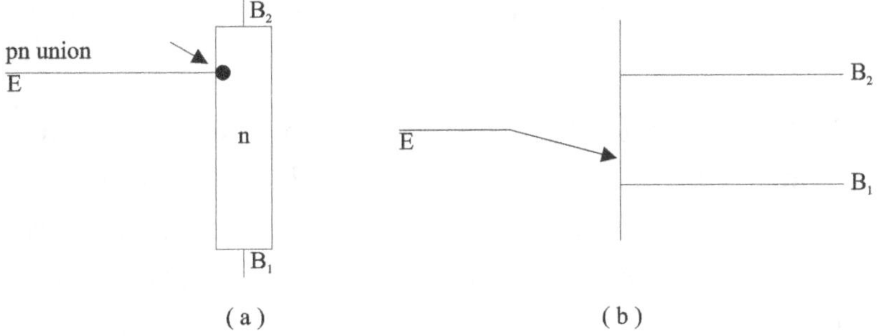

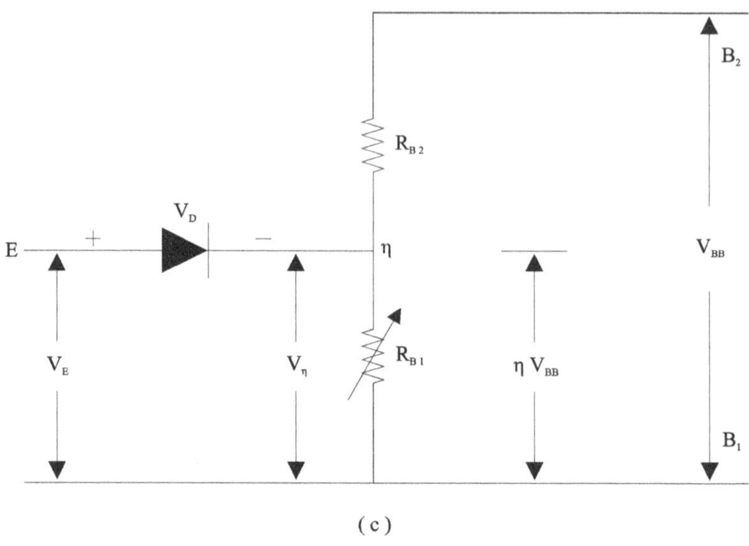

(c)

Figure 4-1 (a) Structure of the UJT (b) Symbol (c) Equivalent circuit of the UJT.

Between B_2 and B_1, there are two resistors, R_{B1} and R_{B2}. The sum of these resistors is equal to the interbase resistance $R_{BB} = R_{B1} + R_{B2}$. Since the resistance R_{B1} varies as a function of the emitter current, I_E, it is represented as a variable resistor (figure 4.1(c)). In the same figure, the voltage V_η at point η with respect to B_1, by voltage division, is:

$$V_\eta = \frac{R_{B1}V_{BB}}{R_{B1} + R_{B2}} \tag{4.1}$$

In the given expression in (4.2).

$$\eta = \frac{R_{B1}}{R_{B1} + R_{B2}} = \frac{R_{B1}}{R_{BB}} \tag{4.2}$$

η is called the intrinsic turn-off ratio.

Therefore, the equation given in (4.1) can be rewritten as:

$$V_\eta = \eta V_{BB} \qquad\qquad (4.3)$$

In Figure 4.2, the basic points can be observed in the manufacturing DC characteristics of the UJT.

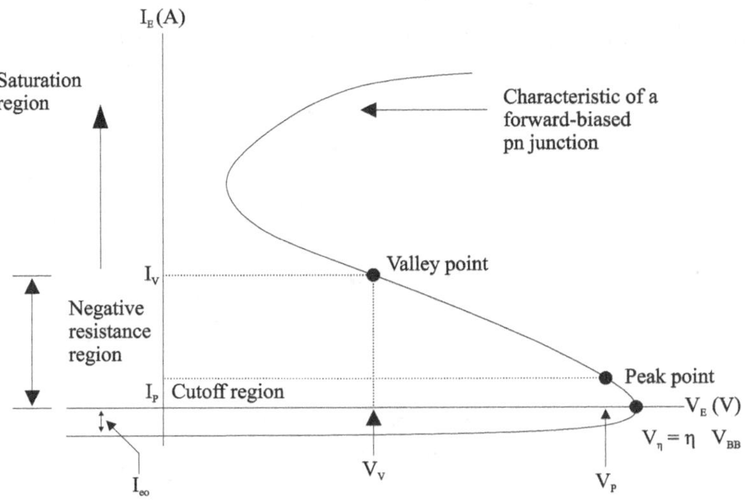

Figure 4-2. UJT current vs. voltage characteristic.

UJT parameters and characteristics

Manufacturers specify a series of characteristic parameters for the device. With these, the user can perform the necessary calculations for any practical design.

Next, we will see the different parameters and the range of values for a particular unijunction transistor: the UJT 2N2646.

- INTRINSIC TURN-OFF RATIO, η.

As defined earlier, it is referred to as:

$$\eta = \frac{R_{B1}}{R_{B1} + R_{B2}} = \frac{R_{B1}}{R_{BB}}$$

Indicate the relationship between the base resistance, B_1, and the total base resistance. In other words, it is the voltage divider attenuation factor.

Its value is measured with $V_{BB} = 10V$. For the 2N2646.

$$\eta_{mín} = 0.56$$
$$\eta_{máx} = 0.75$$
$$\eta_{típ} = 0.69$$

- INTERBASE RESISTANCE, R_{BB}.

It is measured with $V_{BB} = 3V$ and $l_E = 0$.

$$R_{BBmín} = 4.7K\Omega$$
$$R_{BBmáx} = 9.1K\Omega$$

$$R_{BBtíp} = 6.7K\Omega$$

- SATURATION EMITTER VOLTAGE, $V_{E(sat)}$.

This value is given for $V_{BB} = 10V$ and $I_E = 50mA$. It indicates when the $E - B_1$ junction has reached saturation.

$$V_{E(sat)} = 2V$$

- REVERSE SATURATION CURRENT, $I_{E(sat)}$.

It is the current that flows when the $E - B_1$ junction is reverse biased. For $V_{B2-E} = 30V$ and $IB_1 = 0$:

$$I_{E(sat)máx} = 12\mu A$$
$$I_{E(sat)típ} = 0.001\mu A$$

- PEAK EMITTER CURRENT, I_p.

It is the current that appears when the voltage at the emitter is equal to V_p (peak point). It has been measured with $V_{BB} = 25V$.

- VALLEY EMITTER CURRENT, I_V.

With $V_{BB} = 20V$.

$$I_{Vmín} = 4mA$$
$$I_{Vmáx} = 5mA$$

- MAXIMUM RANGES.

Power dissipation: 300mW (referring to V_{BB} and I_{B2}).

$$I_{E(RMS)máx} = 50mA.$$
$$I_{E(pico)máx} = 2A.$$
$$V_{E(inv)máx} = 30V.$$
$$V_{BBmáx} = 35V.$$

- PACKAGE TYPE.

Usually, the UJT is packaged in typical transistor packages, such as TO-5 or TO-18, as shown in Figure 4.3. The notch is always located between E and B_2, and when measured with an ohmmeter, $R_{B1} > R_{B2}$.

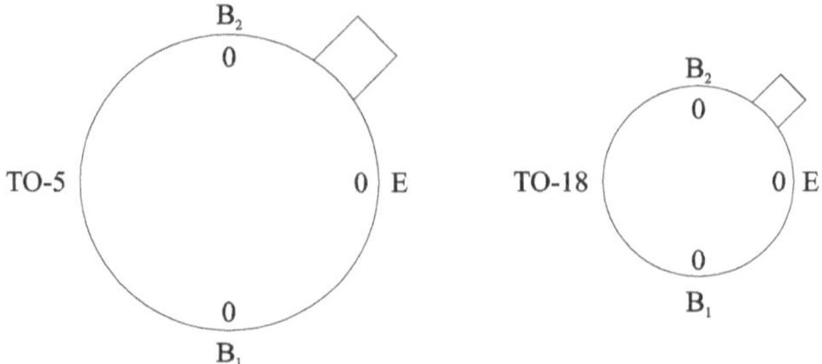

Figure 4-3. Typical UJT packaging.

Relaxation oscillator with UJT

Figure 4.4 shows the basic circuit of a relaxation oscillator with UJT.

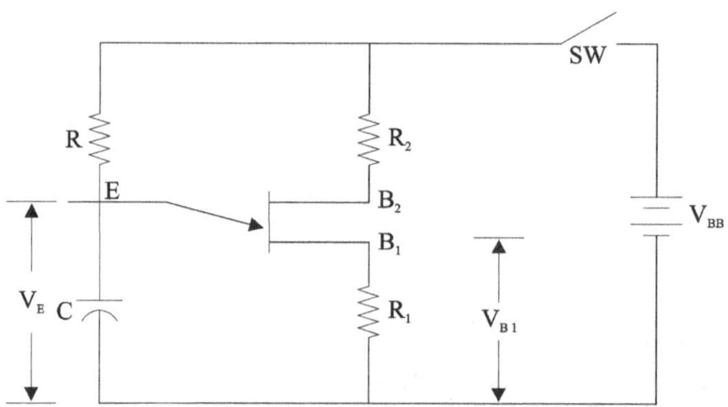

Figure 4-4. Relaxation oscillator circuit with UJT.

Initially, the capacitor is discharged. When the switch is closed, the capacitor starts to charge through R until it reaches the value of V_{BB}. For a value of V_E lower than the peak voltage, the UJT is in the cutoff region. As soon as the capacitor voltage reaches the peak value, V_p, the UJT triggers and R_{B1} decreases to a small value. The capacitor discharges very quickly through R_{B1} and R_1 to ground. But when V_E becomes equal to V_v, the UJT turns off. The capacitor starts to charge again, and as shown in Figure 4.5 (a), the cycle repeats. The resulting waveform across the capacitor is known as a sawtooth wave, and its peak-to-peak amplitude is equal to the difference between the peak and valley voltages $((V_p - V_v))$.

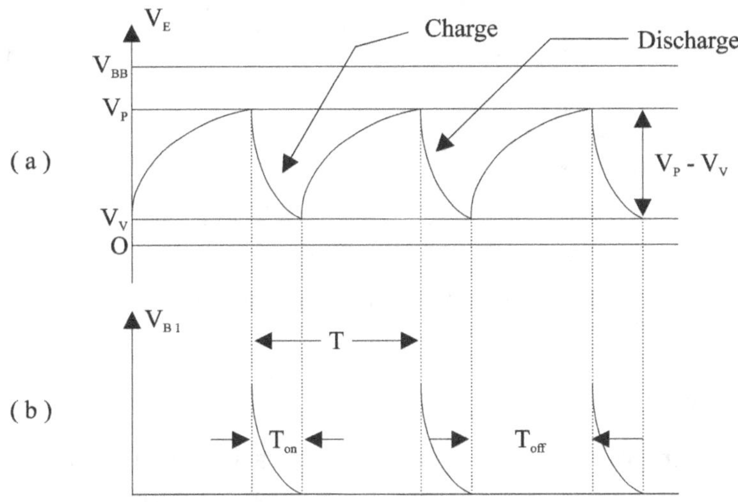

Figure 4-5. Waveforms in the relaxation oscillator (a) in the capacitor (b) in the resistor R1 of Figure 4.4.

The waveform between the terminals of resistor R_1 is shown in Figure 4.5 (b). During the time when C is discharging, a current flows through R_1, producing an appropriate triggering voltage to activate an SCR. The triggering amplitude is determined by the value of R_1, and by modifying the values of C and R, the time between the triggers can be varied. The UJT circuit shown in Figure 4.4 is frequently used as phase control in circuits involving SCRs and TRIACs.

EXAMPLE 4.1.

For the circuit in Figure 4.6, calculate the values of the components. We want the frequency of the signal to be 0.6kHz.

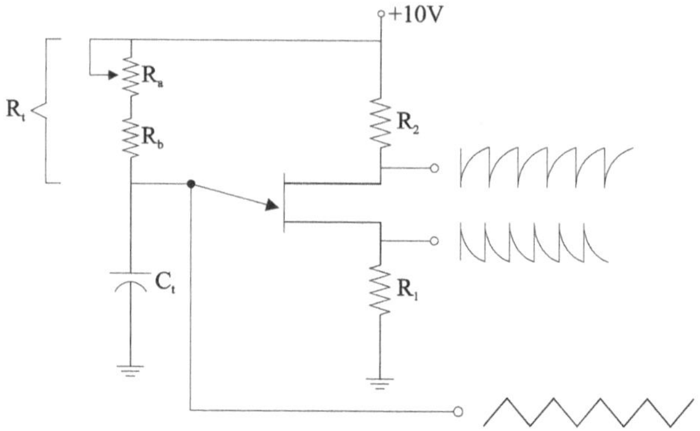

Figure 4-6. Example circuit 4.1. Sawtooth outputs and trigger pulses.

SOLUTION

Whenever you want to design a relaxation oscillator circuit, like the one shown in Figure 4.6, you can follow the following procedure.

The value of R_t can be chosen within the range of.

$$R_{tmín} \leq R_t \leq R_{tmáx}$$

Where:

$$R_{tmín} \geq \frac{V_{BB}}{I_{Vmín}} \qquad y \qquad R_{tmáx} = \frac{V_{CD}(1-\eta_{máx})-V_D}{I_{pmáx}}$$

For a 2N2646 and a direct current bias voltage, $V_{CD} = 10V$, we will have:

$$R_{tmín} \geq \frac{10V}{4(10^{-3})A} = 2.5K\Omega \qquad y$$

$$R_{tmáx} = \frac{10(1 - 0.75) - 0.6}{5(10^{-6})} = 380K\Omega$$

So, the interval will be:

$$2.5K\Omega \leq R_t \leq 380K\Omega$$

Possible criteria for the selection of R_t could be:

$$R_t = \frac{R_{tmáx} + R_{tmín}}{2} \qquad o$$

$$R_t = \sqrt{R_{tmáx} R_{tmín}}$$

But in general, any value within the interval can be chosen.

Since $T = T_{off} + T_{on}$, but $T_{off} \gg T_{on}$, then $T \cong T_{off}$, the turn-off time is calculated as:

$$T_{off} = R_t C_t Ln\left(\frac{1}{1 - \eta_{típ}}\right) = \frac{1}{f}$$

From this equation, we solve for R_t and obtain:

$$R_t = \frac{1}{f C_t Ln\left(\frac{1}{1 - \eta_{típ}}\right)}$$

Since we want the frequency to be 0.6 KHz, let us assume a value of C_t (arbitrarily) as $0.01\mu F$ and calculate the value of R_t as:

$$R_t = \cfrac{1}{0.6(10^3)0.01(10^{-6})Ln\left(\cfrac{1}{1-0.69}\right)}$$

That is to say:

$$R_t = 142.3K\Omega$$

This resistance value is not commercially available. A common commercial value could be 100KΩ, so we choose this value.

For the selected values of C_t and R_t, the actual oscillation frequency that the circuit will have is:

$$f = \cfrac{1}{R_t C_t Ln\left(\cfrac{1}{1-\eta_{tip}}\right)}$$

$$f = \cfrac{1}{100K\Omega(0.01\mu F)Ln\left(\cfrac{1}{1-0.69}\right)}$$

$$f = 0.86KHz$$

And since $R_t = R_a + R_b$, we can choose, for example, R_a (variable resistor) of 50KΩ, and R_b (fixed resistor) of 50KΩ. With the variable resistor, we can achieve the exact desired frequency value (0.6KHz).

Note that if, for example, 100KΩ of variable resistance and 100KΩ of fixed resistance were desired, R_t would be 200KΩ under maximum conditions, a value that falls within the calculated range for R_t. Similarly, the preselected frequency can still be achieved, although the second case would allow for a higher range of frequency variation.

R_2 can always be calculated using the ratio:

$$R_2 = \frac{4000}{V_{DC}}$$

For our particular case:

$$R_2 = \frac{4000}{10} = 400\Omega$$

R_1 is the resistor through which the capacitor will discharge. In general, any value can be chosen for this resistor, including 0Ω (short circuit), although values within the range of 47Ω - 470Ω are recommended.

For the case at hand, we choose $R_1 = 230\Omega$.

Pulse generation and triangular wave generation

Figure 4.6 shows the waveforms obtained at different points in the relaxation oscillator with UJT.

Due to the variety in these waveforms, the relaxation oscillator can be considered as a versatile signal generator, with special properties for applications such as controlling thyristor devices like SCR and TRIAC.

Due to the charging and discharging of the capacitor, the waveform seen at the emitter terminal of the U.J.T can be obtained. This waveform is a ramp that, with the variation of the resistance R_1, can exhibit flattening in the normally exponential shapes, thus achieving a perfectly triangular signal.

The signal due to the discharge of the capacitor will appear across resistor R_1. The waveform will consist of very short-duration, positive pulses with a frequency controlled by the resistors that make up R_t and the capacitor C_t. (Figure 4.5).

If R_1 is small, let us say 10Ω, the capacitor will discharge quickly, and the pulses will become noticeably short in duration. Similarly, the capacitor signal will approximate a perfect ramp waveform.

The 555 timer

The 555 timer is one of the most versatile and amazing devices that designers have produced. Not only does it currently have a wide range of applications, but new uses for it are constantly being discovered. Internally, this device combines a relaxation oscillator, two comparators, an RS flip-flop, and a discharge transistor (Figure 4.7).

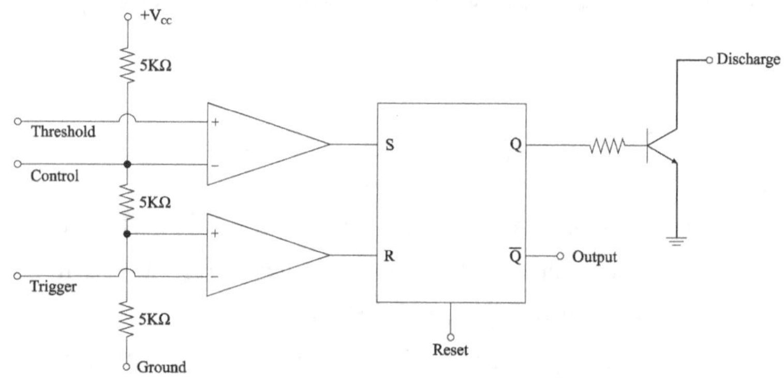

Figure 4-7. Block diagram of the 555 timer.

Figure 4.8 shows the traditional physical layout of the 555. Pin number 1 is located at the top left corner, and the numbering follows a counterclockwise direction.

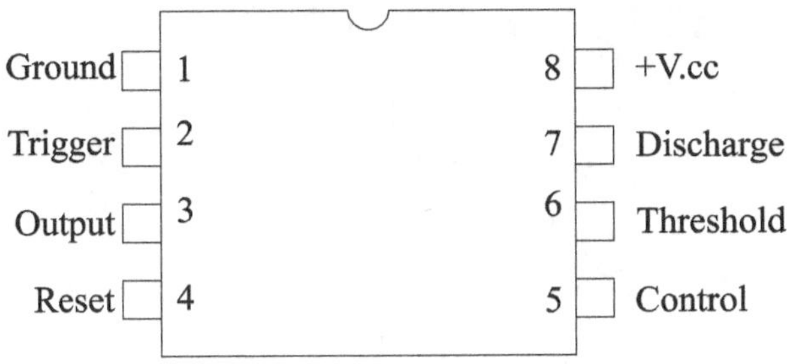

Figure 4-8. Typical 555 packaging.

In figure 4.9 (a), the circuit of a transistor-based flip-flop can be seen. Each collector drives the opposite base through a resistor R_B. In this circuit, while one transistor is saturated, the other is in cutoff. For example, if the right transistor is saturated, its collector voltage is approximately zero. That is, there is no excitation for the base of the left transistor, so it will be in cutoff, and its collector voltage will be approximately $+V_{CC}$. This voltage is what saturates the right transistor. Depending on which transistor is saturated, the output Q will be in logical 1 or 0, which represents the presence or absence of voltage, respectively.

In figure 4.9 (b), the symbol of an RS flip-flop is shown. For any signal (1,0) appearing at the Q terminal, the complement of that signal (0,1) will appear at the $\bar{Q}$ terminal.

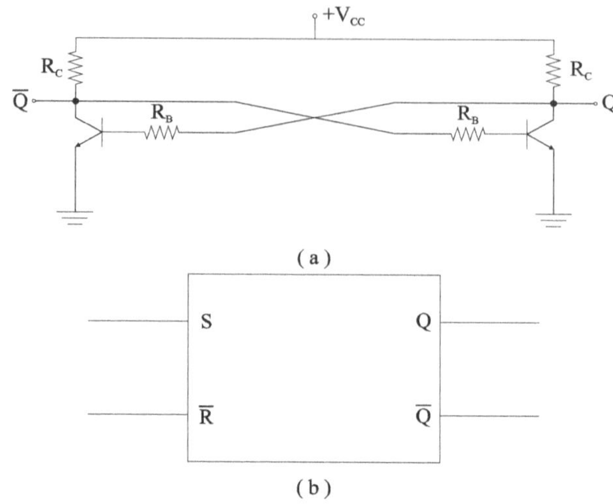

Figure 4-9. (a) Part of a flip-flop RS, (b) Symbol of a flip-flop.

555 clock pulse generator

Figure 4.10 presents the 555 timer as it is commonly used in an electronic circuit. Its operation in this circuit is referred to as astable, and it is often called a free-running multivibrator because it produces a continuous train of rectangular pulses.

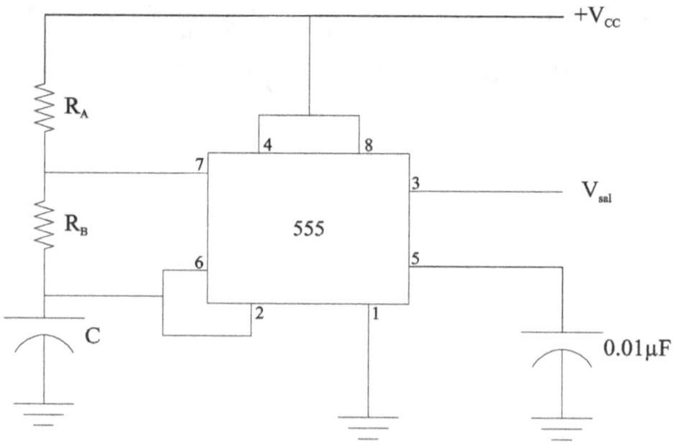

Figure 4-10. Astable timer circuit.

When the output voltage is at a low level, the transistor (see figure 4.7) is in the cutoff region, and the capacitor charges through the equivalent resistance $R_A + R_B$. As a result, the time constant for the capacitor is $(R_A + R_B)C$. As the capacitor charges, the threshold voltage (pin 6) increases. Eventually, it exceeds $+2V_{CC}/3$, and the upper comparator outputs a prominent level, triggering the flip-flop. With the Q output in a high state, the transistor saturates and pulls terminal 7 to ground. Subsequently, the capacitor discharges through R_B. Consequently, the discharge time constant is $R_B C$. When the capacitor voltage decreases slightly below $+V_{CC}/3$, the lower comparator outputs a prominent level, resetting the flip-flop.

Figure 4.11 shows the waveforms as they can be observed at the capacitor and the output, respectively. The output is a square wave. Since the charging time constant is greater than the discharge time constant, the output will not be symmetrical but will have long high states and short low states. The width of the pulses can be varied, if desired, by using potentiometers instead of fixed resistors for R_A and R_B. To determine the extent of asymmetry in the output, we once again use the term duty cycle, and to calculate it, the expression is used.

$$D = \frac{W}{T(100\%)} \tag{4.4}$$

Where:
D = Duty cycle.
W = Pulse width.
T = Signal period.

For example, if $W = 2ms$ and $T = 2.5ms$, then:

$$D = \frac{2ms}{2.5ms}(100\%) = 80\%$$

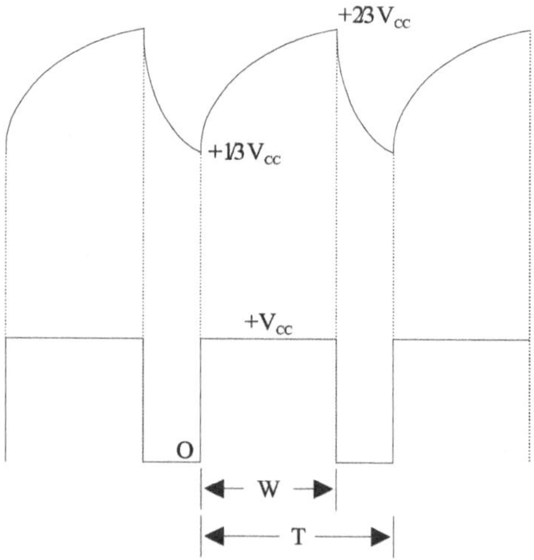

Figure 4-11. Capacitor and output waveforms.

By varying the values of R_A and R_B, the duty cycle can be adjusted between 80% and 100%.

A mathematical solution of the charging and discharging equations provides the following formulas. The output frequency is:

$$f = \frac{1.44}{(R_A + R_B)C} \tag{4.5}$$

And the duty cycle is:

$$D = \frac{R_A + R_B}{(R_A + 2R_B)(100\%)} \tag{4.6}$$

If R_A is much smaller than R_B, the duty cycle approaches 50%.

EXAMPLE 4.2

If in the circuit of Figure 4.12 the potentiometer in R_A is set to 7.5KΩ and the potentiometer R_B is set to 5KΩ, I would determine the frequency of the output signal and the duty cycle. Also, the charging and discharging time of the capacitor.

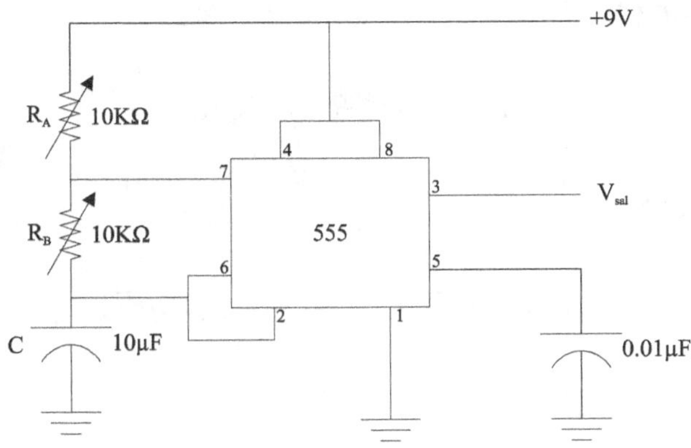

Figure 4-12. Circuit of example 4.2.

SOLUTION

The value of $R_A = 7.5K\Omega$, $R_B = 5K\Omega$, and the capacitor $C = 10\mu F$.

Using equation (4.5) to find the frequency, we have:

$$f = \frac{1.44}{(R_A + R_B)C} = \frac{1.44}{(7.5K\Omega + 5K\Omega)10\mu F}$$

That is:

$$f = 11.52Hz$$

Similarly, if we use equation (4.6), we obtain:

$$D = \frac{R_A + R_B}{R_A + 2R_B}(100\%) = \frac{7.5K\Omega + 5K\Omega}{(7.5K\Omega + 10K\Omega)(100\%)}$$

In other words:

$$D = 71.42\%$$

The charging time of the capacitor is:

$$\tau_{carga} = (R_A + R_B)C$$

Replacing:

$$\tau_{carga} = (7.5K\Omega + 5K\Omega)(10\mu F)$$

That is:

$$\tau_{carga} = 0.125seg$$

And the discharge time is:

$$\tau_{descarga} = R_B C$$

Replacing:

$$\tau_{descarga} = 5K\Omega(10\mu F)$$

That is:

$$\tau_{descarga} = 0.05seg$$

Application of these signals in microprocessors

As already mentioned, there are many applications that can be given to this device. One of them is the *clock circuit*.

The clock circuit is shown in figure 4.10, which provides a signal as seen in the bottom part of figure 4.11. The frequency of the signal, as already noted, depends on the values of R_A and C, and by varying the value of R_B, the frequency can be varied at will.

This signal is particularly useful in microprocessors, where a pulse train needs to be applied to the terminal marked CLOCK (clock). This pulse train is also useful in integrated circuits that require synchronization. The function of the clock circuit is to generate a repetitive pulse of very precise frequency and duration, which is used as a timing signal in synchronous systems, that is, systems or circuits that sequentially share data or devices.

In an integrated circuit, the CLOCK terminal (or clock input) is used to receive a synchronization signal, but in other applications, it can be used for controlling data signals.

Currently, almost all clock generators are crystal-controlled, due to the stability that can be achieved with these devices.

Thyristors

Thyristors constitute a family of silicon semiconductor devices that can be used as switches, as they have two stable operating states: conduction (saturation) and non-conduction (cut-off). This switching is achieved by the thyristor due to its internal feedback. The main application of this family of devices is to control high current values for motors and other high-demand elements.

The most important devices in this family are the silicon-controlled rectifier (SCR) and the bidirectional triode thyristor (TRIAC), which can control power levels that include relatively high currents, up to $2000A$.

Other devices include the programmable unijunction transistor (PUT), the bidirectional diode (DIAC), the four-layer diode (D4), the silicon unilateral switch (SUS), the silicon-controlled switch (SCS), etc. These devices are widely used in control and triggering of power components.

Since the characteristics of thyristors are remarkably similar, the study conducted on one element (such as the SCR, which is the most commonly used) is applicable to all the others.

Thyristor operating principle

All thyristors can be explained using the circuit shown in Figure 4.13 (a). Note that transistor Q_1 is a pnp device, and transistor Q_2 is a npn device. The collector of Q_2 drives the base of Q_1. This circuit allows thyristors to function as switches.

In the circuit of Figure 4.13, if the base current of Q_2 increases, the collector current of Q_2 also increases, leading to more base current flowing through Q_1. This results in a higher collector current in Q_1, further exciting the base of Q_2. These successive increases drive both transistors into saturation, and the circuit behaves like a closed switch, as shown in Figure 4.13 (b).

Similarly, if the base current of Q_2 decreases, the collector current of Q_2 also decreases. This further reduces the base current of Q_2. These successive changes drive the transistors into cutoff, and the circuit behaves like an open switch, as shown in Figure 4.13 (c).

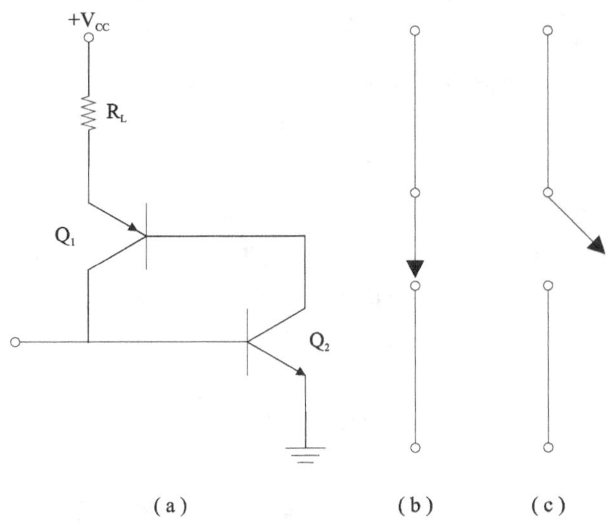

Figure 4-13. Thyristor equivalent circuit with transistors.

If the switch is closed, it remains closed until a change in the currents operates in the circuit; the same applies if the switch is opened, it remains open until a change in it operates a change in the circuit. Due to this type of switching being based on positive feedback, the circuit is called a **latch**.

Switchover of a latch

When we talk about switching of the latch, we are not referring to the specific act of opening and closing the switch.

One way to close the latch is to use a triggering circuit to directly bias the base-emitter diode of Q_2 in Figure 4.13 (a). A single pulse is sufficient, as it activates the circuit currents, and once the currents are present, they take care of the excitation. Another way to close the latch is to apply a high voltage V_{CC} to cause breakdown in any of the collector diodes. This results in collector current flow, equivalent to applying the triggering pulse. The voltage applied for this purpose is referred to as the breakdown voltage.

One way to open the latch is by reducing the load current to zero. This causes the transistors to exit saturation and enter cutoff. For example, in the circuit of Figure 4.13 (a), the load resistor R_L can be opened. Another way to achieve the same effect is by decreasing the voltage V_{CC} to zero. In these cases, a closed latch will open. An additional alternative to open the latch is by applying a reverse pulse. See Figure 4.14.

In summary, we can close a latch:

1. By applying a positive pulse.

2. By applying a high voltage V_{CC}.

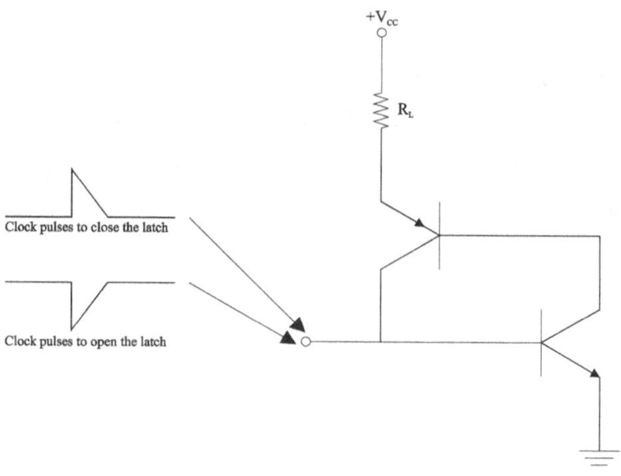

Figure 4-14. Pulses to open or close a latch.

And to open a latch:

1. Reduce the load current to zero (the load resistor can be opened).

2. Decreasing the voltage V_{CC} to zero.

3. Apply a reverse pulse.

SCR (Silicon controlled rectifier)

The silicon-controlled rectifier (SCR) has four alternating layers pnpn, and an extra connection at the base of the npn section, as shown in Figure 4.15.

In Figure 4.16 (a), the latch circuit of the SCR can be seen, and in Figure 4.16 (b), the symbol commonly used to represent it in different circuits is shown.

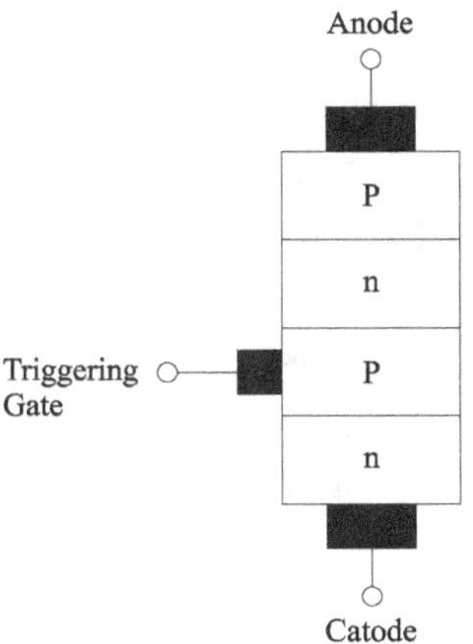

Figure 4-15. Physical constitution of the SCR.

Since the silicon-controlled rectifier is essentially a latch, as discussed in the previous sections, the methods of turning on and off the SCR are considered practically the same as those discussed for the latch.

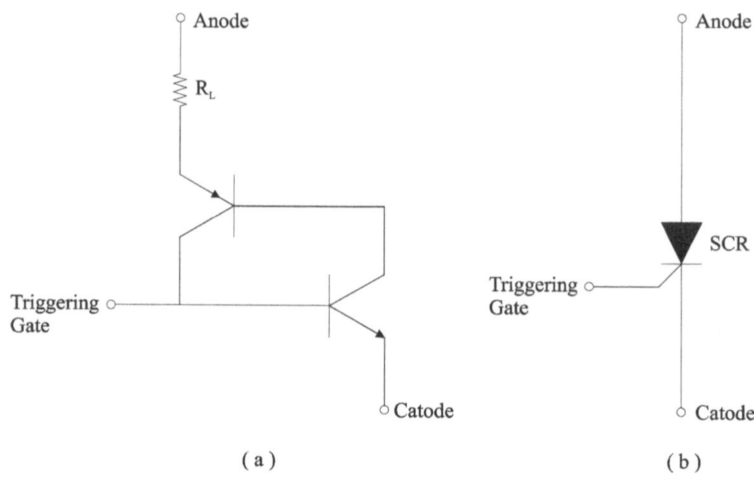

Figure 4-16 (a) Latch circuit (b) SCR symbol.

Now, since the triggering gate of an SCR is essentially a diode, at least 0.7V is required to close it, along with a trigger current on the order of 10mA. Once the SCR is closed, a voltage called the holding voltage appears across its terminals, typically around 1V.

To open or block an SCR, its current must be reduced below the minimum current required for triggering, known as the holding current. This holding current is also on the order of 10mA, although these values can vary considerably depending on the specific references used.

Checking SCRs

Figure 4.17 shows the schematic diagram of an SCR tester. The procedure for checking is as follows: quickly touch the gate of the SCR with the cable connected to the 1K resistor. The LED should light up and remain in that state, indicating that current is flowing through the circuit. To turn off the LED again, disconnect the battery supply, and to turn it on again, follow the procedure described above.

With this tester, we observe that an SCR conducts when a positive voltage is applied to the gate, and it continues to conduct even when the gate voltage is removed.

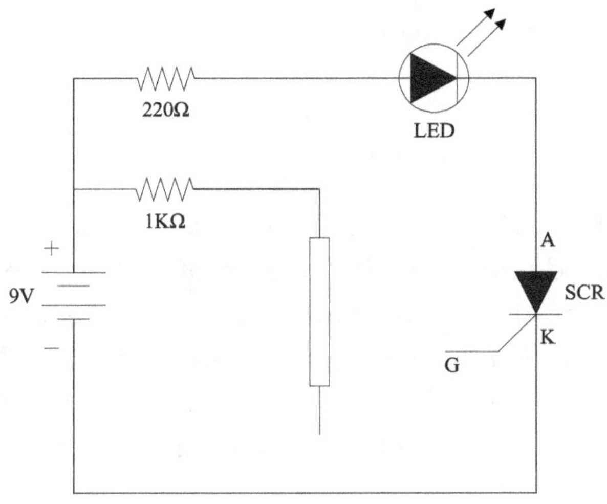

Figure 4-17. SCR Tester.

The TRIAC (Two-way triad)

The TRIAC is a device that functions as two silicon-controlled rectifiers connected in parallel, which allows it to control current in both directions. The best way to trigger a TRIAC is to apply a pulse of forward bias to the gate. Figure 4.18 shows the symbol used to represent a TRIAC.

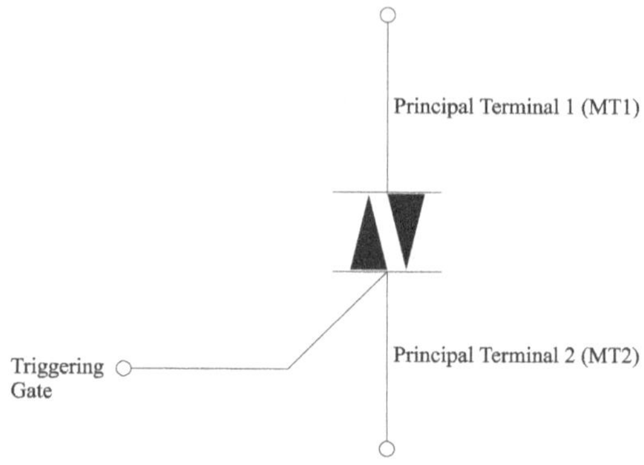

Figure 4-18. TRIAC symbol.

Since the TRIAC is a bidirectional device, it does not have an anode and cathode like an SCR, for example. The terminals for the main conduction path are called main terminal 1 and main terminal 2, represented as MT1 and MT2 (Figure 4.18). The gate is associated with MT1, with polarities and trigger levels indicated in relation to MT1.

The DIAC

In Figure 4.19, the symbols commonly used to represent a DIAC can be observed. The way to make a DIAC enter conduction is to exceed the breakdown voltage value between its terminals in either direction.

Once the DIAC is conducting, the only way to turn it off is through current decrease blocking. In other words, the current must be reduced to a value below the device's holding current.

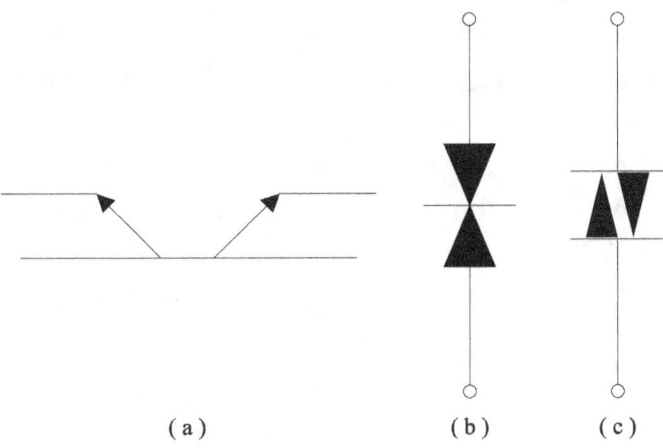

Figure 4-19. Symbols for a DIAC.

In Figure 4.20, a relaxation oscillator complemented with an SCR can be observed to control the operation of a load. The load, in this case, can be a light bulb or a low-power motor.

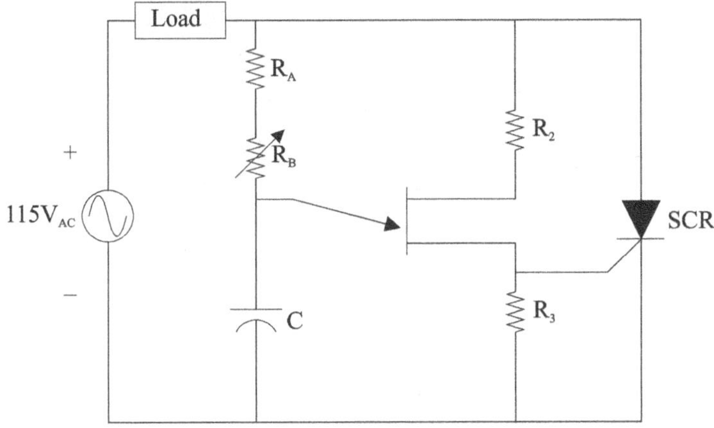

Figure 4-20. Relaxation oscillator supplemented with SCR to control a load.

The QUADRAC

In Figure 4.21, a circuit can be observed to control a load using a TRIAC triggered by a DIAC. The circuit can be implemented using the two mentioned devices. However, for this purpose, a quadrac can also be used. This is a device that internally combines the TRIAC and the DIAC, as seen in Figure 4.21. To activate and deactivate it, the procedure is similar to what was seen for the SCR and the TRIAC.

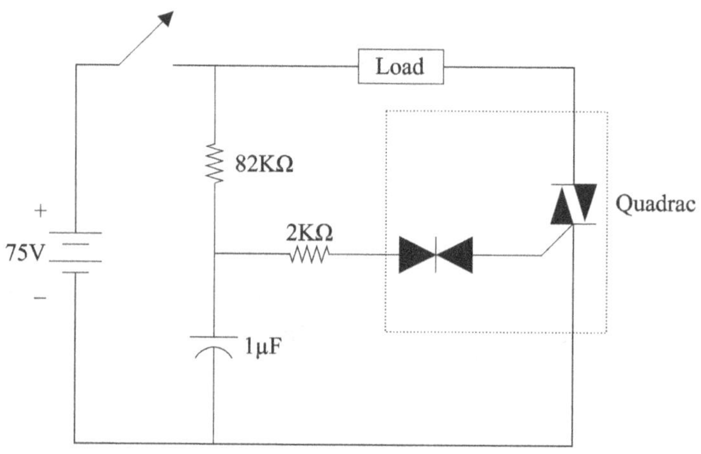

Figure 4-21. Control of a load by means of a CUADRAC.

TTL and CMOS logic families

For digital integrated circuits belonging to the Transistor-Transistor Logic (TTL) family, the power supply voltage should be 5V and must not exceed the value of 5.25V under any circumstances. The source used for circuit operation should be regulated to prevent variations in an unregulated power supply from damaging the integrated circuits.

The signals used for circuit operation must only be within the range of 0V to 5V and should not exceed 5V or have negative values below 0V.

In the connections of these integrated circuits, it is advisable to avoid exceedingly long wiring. If it is not possible for the power source to be close to the integrated circuits, it is convenient to place coupling capacitors, preferably tantalum capacitors with a value of 1 to 10µF, next to them.

For digital integrated circuits belonging to the CMOS (Complementary Metal-Oxide-Semiconductor) family, the power supply voltage can range from 3V to 15V. However, it is recommended to power them with values of 5V, 6V, 9V, or 12V, always sourced from a regulated power supply. Since the current consumption of these circuits is low, they can also be powered using batteries.

The signal voltages must not exceed the positive supply level and should not have negative values below 0V. It is recommended to never connect an input signal to a CMOS circuit when it does not have a power supply voltage.

Precautions

Due to the construction of the transistors used in CMOS integrated circuits, their input terminals are overly sensitive as they operate with currents in the range of picoamperes.

For this reason, it is easy for these transistors to be damaged by static electricity that may be present on our hands at a given moment. To prevent this from happening, it is important to avoid touching the terminals of the integrated circuits or storing them in places where static electricity may be present.

REVIEW

Concepts

Define or discuss the following:
- Special device.
- Unijunction transistor.
- Intrinsic turn-off ratio of UJT.
- Relaxation oscillator.
- 555 timer.
- Flip-flop.
- Clock pulse generator with 555.
- Duty cycle of a signal.
- Synchronous circuit or system.
- Thyristor.
- Latch.
- Closure of a latch.
- Opening of a latch.
- SCR.
- TRIAC.
- DIAC.
- CUADRAC.
- TTL logic family.
- CMOS logic family.

EXERCISES

4.1.   Based on the procedure followed in example 4.1, determine the values of the components in the circuit shown in figure 4.22 if the voltage value $V_{CC} = +15V$ and $f = 0.8KHz$.

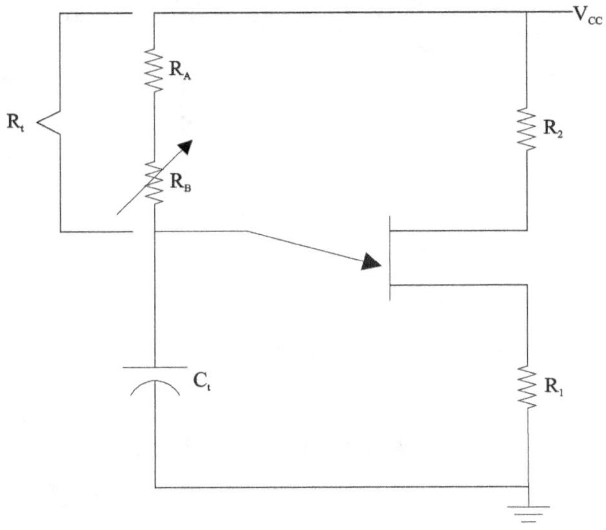

Figure 4-22. Circuit of exercise 4.1.

4.2.   Repeat the previous exercise, but if the bias voltage $V_{CC} = 15V$ and $f = 0.95KHz$.

4.3.   In the circuit of figure 4.23, the potentiometer in R_A has a maximum value of $10K\Omega$. If a fixed resistance of $5K\Omega$ is placed in R_B and a capacitor of $4.7\mu F$ is placed in C_t, determine the frequency of the output signal and the duty cycle when the potentiometer in R_A is set to (a) minimum, (b) mid-value, (c) maximum. Also, determine the charging and discharging time of the capacitor for each case.

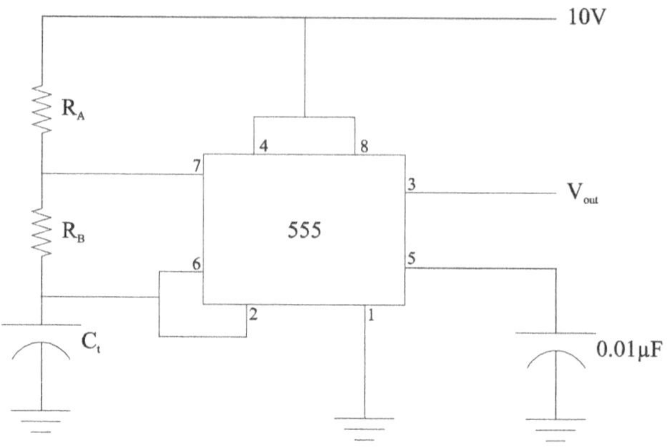

Figure 4-23. Circuit of exercise 4.3.

Chapter 5
ACADEMIC SUPPORT GUIDE

This chapter aims to be an academic support guide for laboratory practices. It is essentially a working manual that presents specific objectives, a step-by-step procedure, and a questionnaire for evaluation. The evaluation covers not only the practical achievements but also the assimilation of the concepts discussed.

Many of the circuits presented throughout the text can be easily implemented; in fact, some of the setups shown closely resemble certain circuits studied earlier. This is mainly done to reinforce the concepts based on these circuits and highlight their importance in the overall management of components and electronic circuits. Each practice is designed to be conducted within a module of either 3 hours and 45 minutes or even 2 hours and 60 minutes. During the practice, the requested data should be recorded according to the work guide, and a report should be prepared containing the assembled circuits, collected data, result tables, and conclusions.

It would be ideal to have a cathode ray oscilloscope for observing waveforms in the various circuits. However, if one is not available, all other steps should be performed, taking measurements with a preferably digital multimeter. The report should be presented using these measurements.

142

PRACTICE N°1

DIFFERENTIAL AMPLIFIER

GOALS

1. Characterize the amplifier as a discrete component-based element.

2. Verify the importance of having the amplifier differential components with the same operating characteristics.

PROCEDURE

1. Build the circuit shown in Figure 5.1.1 with two identical transistors.

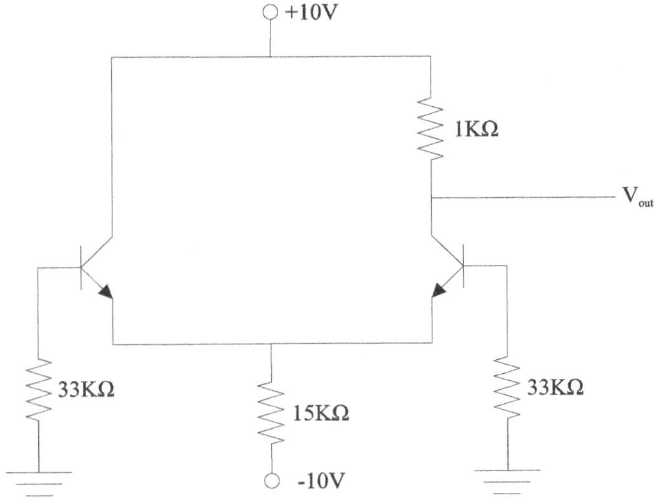

Figure 5-1-1. Discrete differential amplifier.

2. Measure the output voltage and the voltages across the base resistors.

3. Repeat the setup, but this time with two different transistors, and measure the output voltage and the base voltages again. Do they vary compared to the previous case?

4. Assemble the circuit shown in Figure 5.1.2 and determine the relationship between the output voltage and the input voltage.

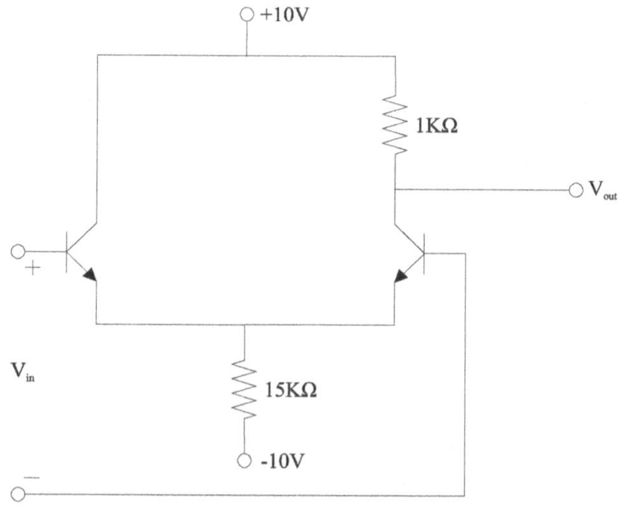

Figure 5-1-2. Discrete differential amplifier.

REPORT

1. Record the results in a table.

2. Analyze the results.

3. Present your conclusions.

QUESTIONS

1. In the circuit of figure 5.1.1, do you observe any changes when using transistors with distinct characteristics?

2. Does the circuit in figure 5.1.2 function as a good amplifier?

PRACTICE N°2

INVERTING AND NON-INVERTING AMPLIFIER

GOALS

1. Characterize the operational amplifier as a phase-shifting device.

2. Verify the signal summation effect of an operational amplifier.

PROCEDURE

1. Assemble the circuits shown in Figure 5.2.1 (a) and (b) and observe the input signal and output signal with the oscilloscope. With the channel selector set to DUAL, observe the superposition of the input and output signals.

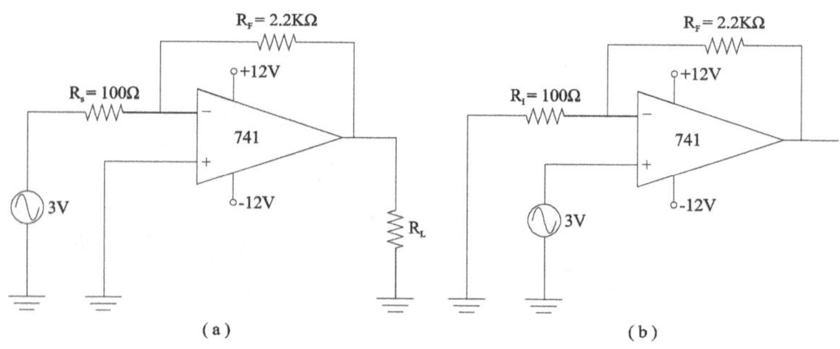

Figure 5-2-1. Amplifier (a) inverting, (b) non-inverting.

2. Replace the feedback resistors (R_f) with 5KΩ potentiometers and vary them while observing the output signal. Take five different points for this purpose (for example, 1K, 2K, 3K, 4K, 5K).

REPORT

1. Record the observed waveforms on the oscilloscope along with their corresponding measured values.

2. For the second point, create a table of results.

3. Analyze the obtained results.

4. Present your conclusions.

PRACTICE N°3

OFFSET VOLTAGE OF AN OPERATIONAL AMPLIFIER

GOALS

1. Characterize the operational amplifier as an integrated circuit.

2. Verify the concept of offset voltage.

3. Understand the methods for compensating offset voltage.

PROCEDURE

1. Assemble the circuit shown in Figure 5.3.1 using an LM741 operational amplifier and measure the output offset voltage.

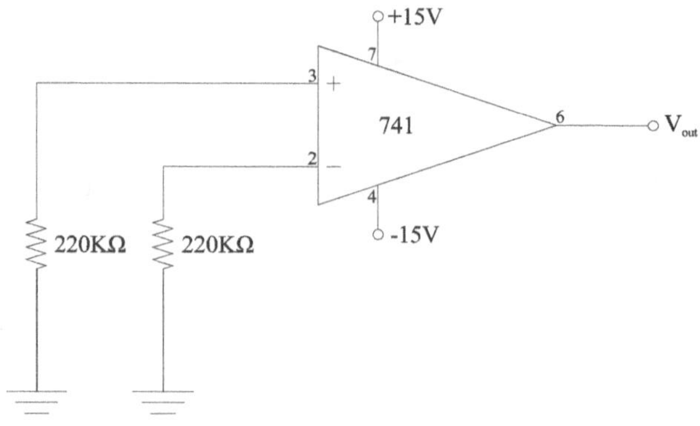

Figure 5-3-1. Circuit to determine the offset voltage.

2. Assemble the circuit shown in Figure 5.3.2 and verify that the offset voltage is canceled for some position of the potentiometer.

3. Repeat the previous procedure but use a different type of operational amplifier (such as LM11C or LM324) for this purpose).

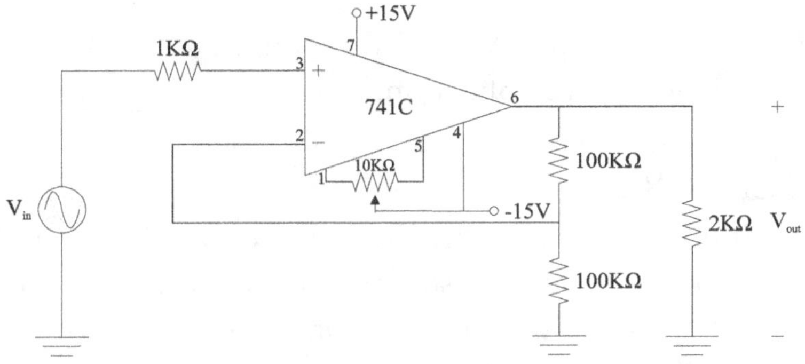

Figure 5-3-2. Circuit with output offset voltage cancellation.

REPORT

1. Present a table with the results.

2. Analyze the obtained results.

3. Present your conclusions.

QUESTIONS

1. Does the offset voltage vary from one amplifier reference to another?

2. Are significant changes observed when varying the value of the potentiometer in the circuit of Figure 5.3.2?

PRACTICE N°4

OPERATIONAL AMPLIFIER AS AN ADDER

GOALS

1. Characterize the operational amplifier as a computing element.

2. Verify the operation of the operational amplifier in this practical application.

PROCEDURE

1. Build the circuits shown in Figure 5.4.1 (a) and (b), applying small sinusoidal signals (1V, 2V, 3V) at the inputs, and limit the current with resistors below 470Ω. For feedback, use resistor values greater than 1K.

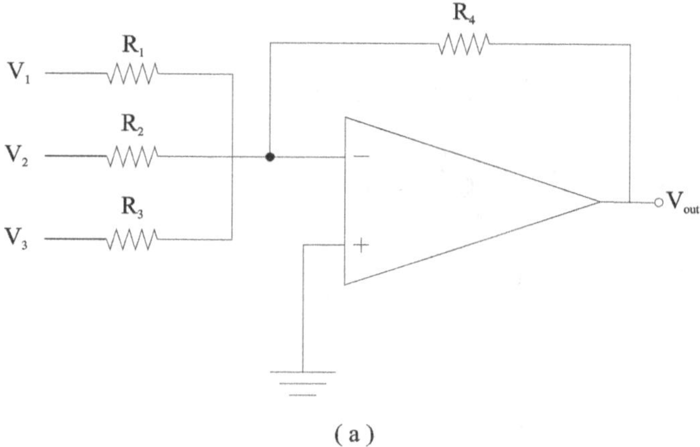

(a)

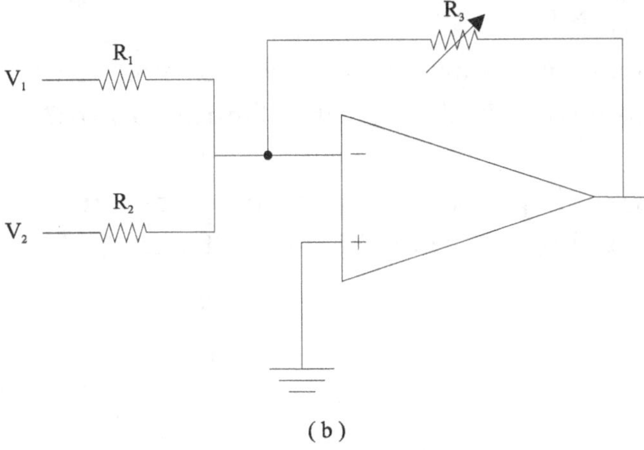

(b)

Figure 5-4-1. Three-input (a) summing amplifier (b) two-input (c) two-input amplifier.

2. Observe the input and output signals.

3. In circuit 5.4.1 (b), vary the potentiometer and observe how the output signal changes.

4. In the circuit of Figure 5.4.1 (b), place a sinusoidal signal on V_1 and a square wave signal on V_2. Observe the output signal for this case.

REPORT

1. Draw the observed signals and place their respective values.

2. Create a table with the obtained results.

3. Analyze the results.

4. Present your conclusions.

QUESTIONS

1. Does the square wave have any effect on the sinusoidal wave in the circuit of Figure 5.4.1 (b)?

2. What happens to the output waveform when its magnitude exceeds the bias voltage?

PRACTICE N°5

COMPARATOR, INTEGRATOR, DIFFERENTIA-TOR

GOALS

1. Characterize the operational amplifier as a comparator, integrator, and differentiator.

2. Use these circuits as generators of square, triangular, and pulse waves.

PROCEDURE

1. Build the circuit shown in Figure 5.5.1, applying a 3V sinusoidal signal to the input, and observe the waveforms of both the input and output.

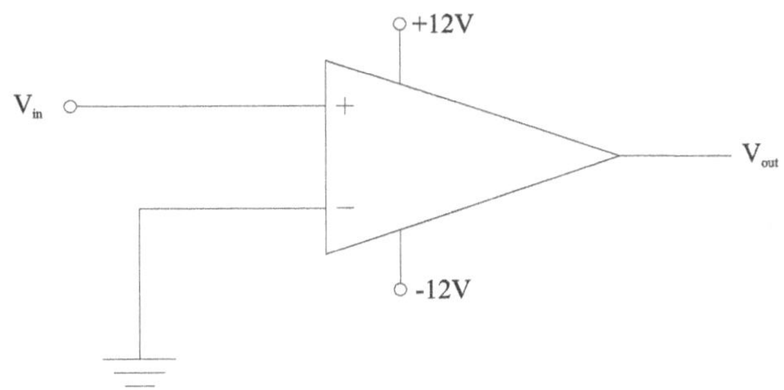

Figure 5-5-1. Operational amplifier used as comparator.

2. Remove the negative power supply (-V) of the amplifier and connect this terminal to ground. Observe the output signal and compare it with the previous exercise.

3. Build the circuit shown in Figure 5.5.2.

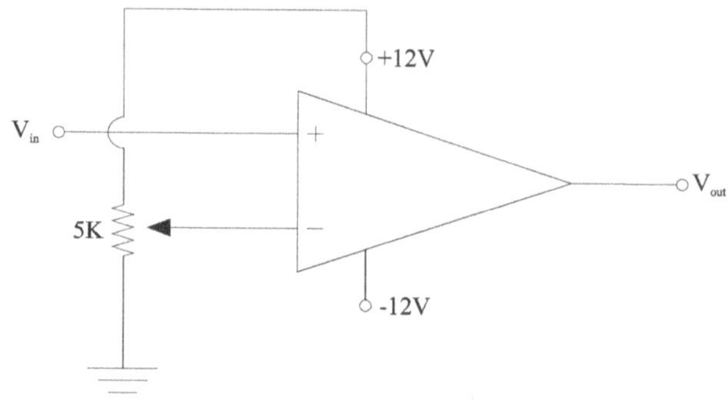

Figure 5-5-2. Comparator as variable frequency rectangular wave generator.

4. Observe the input and output signals for various positions of the potentiometer.

5. Build the circuits shown in Figure 5.5.3 (a) and (b).

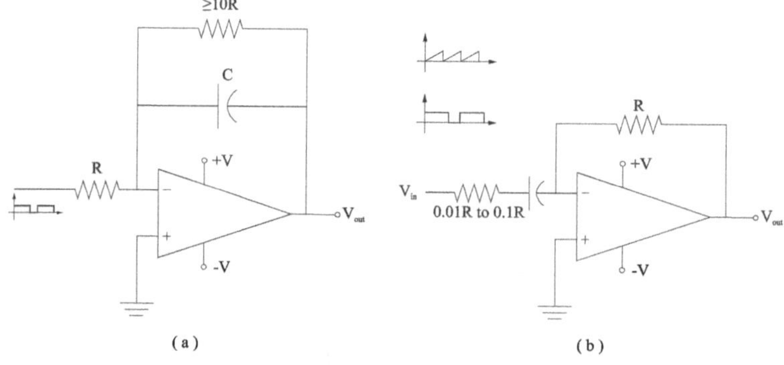

Figure 5-5-3. Operational amplifier as (a) integrator and (b) differentiator.

6. Apply the indicated waveforms to the input and observe both the input and output signals.

REPORT

1. Draw the waveforms with their respective values.

2. Analyze the obtained results and compare them with the expected ones according to the theoretical concepts.

3. Present your conclusions.

PRACTICE N°6

WAVEFORM GENERATORS

GOALS

1. Identify the main signal generator circuits, as well as the most useful waveforms that can be obtained with them.

   Note: Remember that a comparator is a practical and efficient way to convert a sinusoidal signal into a square wave, while an integrator converts it into a triangular wave, and a differentiator reverses the process.

PROCEDURE

1. Build the circuit shown in Figure 5.6.1. (Schmitt Trigger).

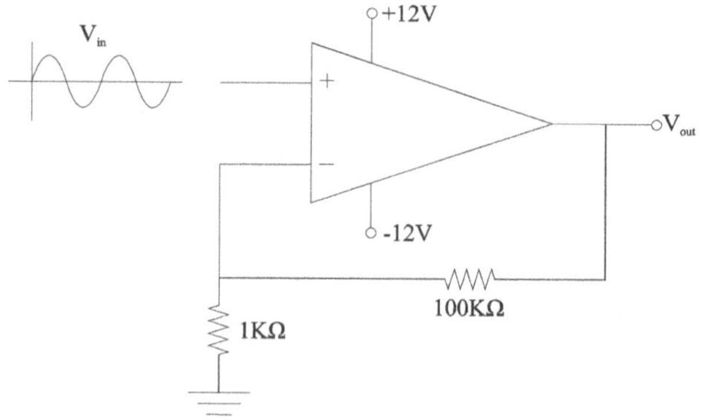

Figure 5-6-1. Sine to square wave converter.

2. Apply a sinusoidal waveform to the circuit and observe both the input and output waveforms, indi-

vidually and then with the channel selector in the DUAL position. Take note of the values for each of the applied signals.

3. Assemble the circuit shown in figure 5.6.2.

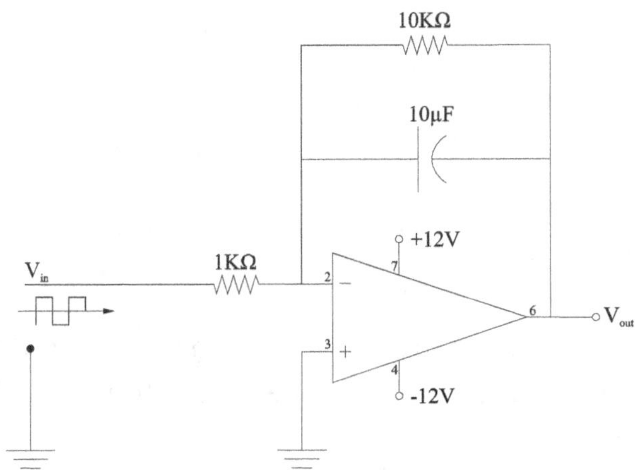

Figure 5-6-2. Square to triangular wave converter.

4. Apply a square wave signal (using the circuit from figure 5.6.1) and repeat the process described in step 2.

5. Assemble the circuit shown in figure 5.6.3.

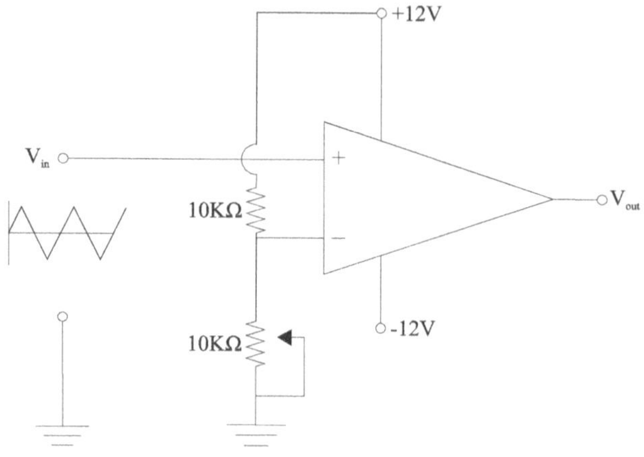

Figure 5-6-3. Triangle wave to pulse converter.

6. Apply a triangular wave signal (using the circuit shown in figure 5.6.2) and repeat the procedure outlined in step 2.

REPORT

1. Draw the complete circuit that you obtained at the end of the practice (in cascade).

2. Draw the waveforms that you observed for each case, along with the respective values measured on the oscilloscope.

3. Analyze the obtained signals.

4. Present your conclusions.

QUESTIONS

1. What would happen to the waveforms in the different circuits if instead of connecting the terminals 4 of the amplifiers to -V, they were grounded?

PRACTICE N°7

555 TIMER

GOALS

1. Familiarize yourself with one of the most versatile integrated circuits available in the market (the 555).

2. Verify the operation of the 555 as a timer circuit.

3. Visualize the clock pulse waveform obtained through stable operation of the 555 (oscillator).

PROCEDURE

1. Build the circuit shown in Figure 5.7.1.

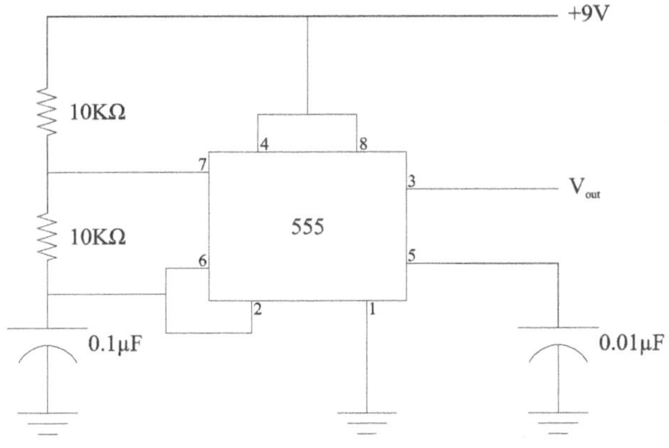

Figure 5-7-1. Astable timer circuit.

2. Observe the waveforms that appear at pin 3 of the 555 (V_{sal}) and across the 0.1µF capacitor. With the channel selector set to DUAL, observe the superposition of both signals. Describe what you see on the screen.

3. Mount the circuit shown in Figure 5.7.2. Observe the signals at the capacitor and at pins 3 (V_{sal}) and 5 of the 555 timer. With the channel selector set to DUAL, simultaneously observe the voltage across the capacitor and pin 5.

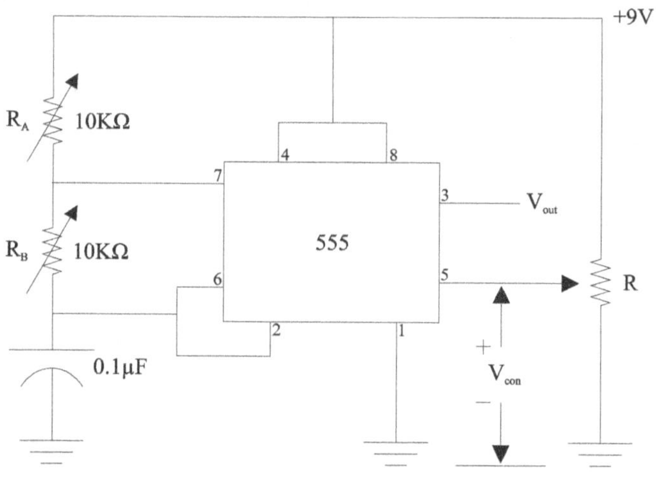

Figure 5-7-2. Voltage controlled oscillator.

REPORT

1. Draw the waveforms observed in each case, along with their respective values.

2. Analyze the observed signals and the results.

3. Present your conclusions.

QUESTIONS

1. What practical applications do you find for these circuits?

2. What happens to the observed signals when the 10K control potentiometers are varied?

PRACTICE N°8

THE SINGLE-JUNCTION TRANSISTOR

GOALS

1. Understand the junction field-effect transistor (JFET).

2. Apply the UJT as a waveform and pulse generator for triggering thyristors.

PROCEDURE

1. Mount the circuit shown in Figure 5.8.1, and using the oscilloscope, observe the waveforms that appear at the capacitor and at the points marked as V_1 and V_2.

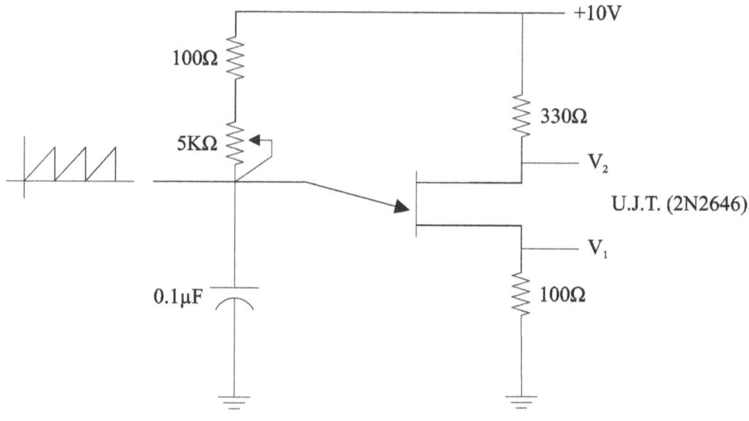

Figure 5-8-1. Sawtooth generator.

2. Short-circuit the 100Ω resistor and observe the signals mentioned above again.

3. Build the circuit shown in Figure 5.8.2 and observe its operation. Try to explain it. What is the requirement for the transistor to saturate? Observe signals.

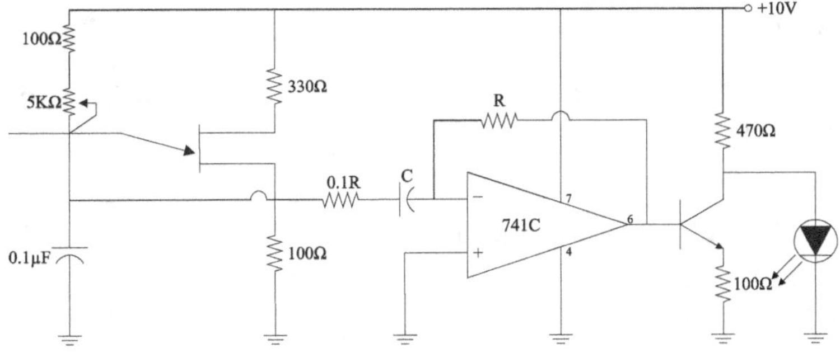

Figure 5-8-2. Relaxation oscillator with UJT.

REPORT

1. Draw the graphs you observed in the circuit with their respective values.

2. Analyze the results obtained.

3. Present your conclusions.

QUESTIONS

1. What applications do you find for the signals observed at the different terminals of the previous circuits?

PRACTICE N°9

POWER CONTROL

GOALS

1. Apply the unijunction transistor in triggering an SCR.

2. Observe the waveform of a power control.

PROCEDURE

1. Assemble the circuit shown in Figure 5.9.1.

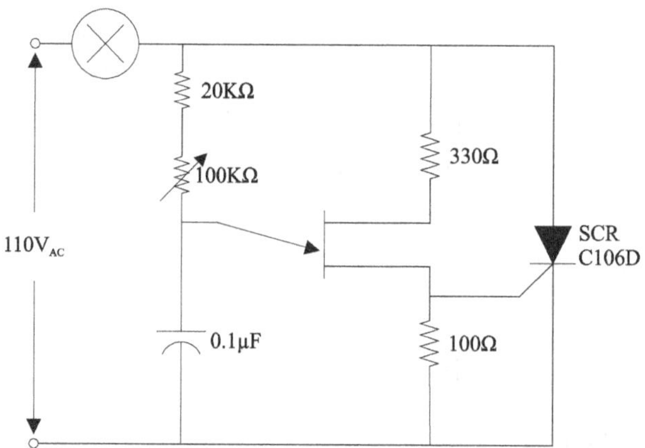

Figure 5-9-1. Control of an SCR by means of UJT.

2. Vary the potentiometer and observe what happens to the bulb. Use the oscilloscope to determine the waveforms at the bulb and the SCR.

3. Assemble the circuit shown in Figure 5.9.2.

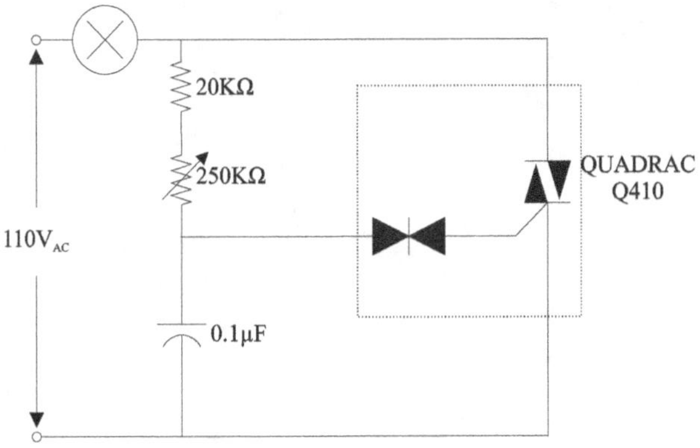

Figure 5-9-2. Power control with CUADRAC.

4. Repeat the procedure outlined in step 2.

REPORT

1. Draw the observed waveforms with their respective values.

2. Describe the operation of both circuits.

3. Analyze the results.

4. Present your conclusions.

GLOSSARY

Amplifier: Circuit that can increase the voltage, current, or power of a signal.

Voltage amplifier: Amplifier that produces maximum voltage gain.

Differential amplifier: Circuit with two transistors whose output is an amplified signal relative to the differential input between the two bases.

Voltage inverting amplifier: Amplifier that has an output with inverted phase relative to the phase of the input signal.

Voltage non-inverting amplifier: Amplifier that has an output with the same phase as the input signal.

Operational amplifier: High-gain voltage amplifier usable for frequencies from 0 to over 2MHz.

Amplitude: Size of a signal, usually its peak value.

Schmitt trigger: Comparator with two switching points. It is immune to noise voltages for peak-to-peak values set by the switching points.

Monolithic IC: Integrated circuit manufactured entirely on a chip.

Thin-film and thick-film IC: Integrated circuit that combines monolithic ICs and discrete components.

Hybrid IC: Combination of monolithic, thin-film, and thick-film ICs.

Duty cycle: Width of a pulse divided by the period of the pulse signal. It is usually multiplied by 100 to obtain a percentage response.

Discrete circuit: Circuit whose components such as resistors, capacitors, transistors, etc., have been soldered or connected in some way.

Integrated circuit: Encapsulated circuit that contains its own resistors, transistors, and diodes. Its size is comparable to that of a single discrete transistor.

Comparator: Circuit that compares two signals, one taken as a reference. The output is a high or low level. The reference voltage is also called the switching point.

Hold current: Minimum current that must flow in a thyristor to keep it in the conduction region.

Short circuit: Occurs when a resistor takes a value of approximately zero ohms. Thus, the voltage will also be close to zero.

Short-circuit output current: Maximum output current that an operational amplifier can deliver for a zero-load resistance.

Inverting input: In an operational amplifier, the input that produces an inverted output.

Non-inverting input: In an operational amplifier, the input that produces an in-phase output.

Cascade stages: Connection of two or more stages in such a way that the output of one stage becomes the input of the next stage.

Frequency: Number of times a signal repeats completely in a unit of time.

Loop gain: Product of the differential voltage gain G and the feedback fraction B. The value of this product is generally large.

Closed-loop gain: Ratio between the differential voltage gain G and the absolute value of the complement to one of the loop gain GB.

Voltage gain: Ratio between the output voltage and the input voltage. The value indicates how much the signal is amplified.

Voltage gain in decibels: Voltage gain that is 20 times the logarithm of the normal voltage.

Measured voltage gain: Voltage gain calculated from the measured values of the input and output voltages.

Predicted voltage gain: Voltage gain calculated from the component values shown in an electrical diagram.

Integrator: Circuit that performs the mathematical operation of integration. A popular application is generating ramp functions from step signals.

Latch: Two transistors connected with positive feedback to simulate the action of a thyristor.

LSI: Large-scale integration. Integrated circuits with more than 100 integrated components.

Virtual ground: Certain type of ground that appears at the inverting terminal of an operational amplifier with negative feedback. It is called virtual ground because it produces some but not all effects of a physical ground. Specifically, it is voltage ground and not current ground. The virtual ground has both zero voltage and zero current.

MSI: Medium-scale integration. Circuits that have 10 to 100 integrated components.

Relaxation oscillator: Circuit that generates an output signal without an input signal. This type of circuit is based on the charging and discharging of a capacitor through a resistor.

Period: Time it takes for a signal to complete one cycle.

Voltage feedback: Type of feedback in which part of the output voltage is applied to the input of the operational amplifier.

Negative feedback: Use of an output signal to feed back into the input of an amplifier. The feedback signal has the opposite phase to the input signal.

Positive feedback: Circuit in which the output signal reinforces, with the same phase, the input signal.

Silicon-Controlled Rectifier (SCR): Three-terminal semiconductor device, anode, cathode, and gate. The SCR is activated by the gate. Once the SCR enters conduction, it is necessary to reduce the current below the holding current to deactivate it. It only conducts in one direction.

Load resistor: Resistor connected to the output of a circuit in order to supply it with voltage and current.

Unity follower: Amplifier used to isolate two circuits when one of them overloads the other. A unity follower amplifier has high input impedance, low output impedance, and a gain of 1. This means that the unity follower passes the signal from one circuit to another without changing it.

SSI: Small-scale integration. Integrated circuits with less than 10 integrated components.

Adder: Circuit with operational amplifier whose output voltage is the sum of two or more input voltages with their respective amplification.

Input offset voltage: If the two input terminals of an amplifier are grounded, a small voltage, called output offset voltage, still appears at the output. The input offset voltage is the voltage that must be applied to the input to eliminate the output offset voltage.

Output offset voltage: Any difference between the output voltage and the ideal output voltage.

Peak voltage: The largest instantaneous value of a voltage that varies with time.

Reference voltage: Very stable and precise voltage of a fixed value taken to be compared with another voltage.

Thyristor: Four-layer semiconductor device that acts as a latch.

Unijunction transistor: Abbreviated UJT. It is a low-power thyristor used for wave generation and other applications.

Triac: Thyristor that can conduct in both directions. It is used to control large alternating currents. It is equivalent to two SCRs in parallel with opposite polarities.

INDEX OF FIGURES

ALBEIRO PATIÑO BUILES

Electrical engineer. With specializations in Literary Hermeneutics and High Management; also, Master in Strategic Management, Planning and Management Control of the IEE of Spain. He has received numerous awards, including first place in the II National Novel Award - National Culture Awards of the University of Antioquia (2006) and first place in the First Short Story Competition of the Association of Employees of the Colombian Industrial Bank (1996). His literary publications are: *Historias cruzadas* (short stories, 1994), *Bandidos y hackers* (novel, 2007), *Phishing* (novel, 2010), *Construir una novela. Cómo orientarse en el proceso de creación literaria* (essay, 2011), *Intimidación* (novel, 2014), *Galán, crónica de un magnicidio* (novel, 2014), *Las intermitencias del corazón I. Melancolía y enajenación* (novel, 2016), *La forja de un escritor* (essay, 2017), *Sombras en la Red* (novel, 2019) and *Las intermitencias del corazón ll. Celos y dolor* (novel, 2019).

Science and Technology

2023

9 789585 395497